SHOES

SHOES

A Play of Fiction and Fact by

NORMAN H DONALDSON

The Pentland Press
Edinburgh – Cambridge – Durham – USA

First published in 1996 by
The Pentland Press Ltd
1 Hutton Close,
South Church
Bishop Auckland
Durham

ISBN 1-85821-351-7

Typeset by Carnegie Publishing, 18 Maynard St, Preston
Printed and bound by Antony Rowe Ltd, Chippenham

This play is dedicated to
the victims of the Holocaust

Never must we forget the six million.
It must never happen again.

Evil dealt with daily becomes familiar, even ordinary.

'No power in Heaven and Earth will erase this shame from my Country — not in Generations — not in Centuries.'

Spoken by Hans Fritzche, German Newscaster in Goebbel's Propaganda Ministry, at the Nurenberg Trials in which he was a defendant.

The Characters

Louie
Hans
Steiner
Hoess
Kleinsmidt
Möller
Brukmann
Steiner Snr.
Inmates
SS Guards

Author's note

THERE are no defined acts in this play. The action in the play is supported through each scene by controlled variations of light, either strong or weak, or focused, or shafted, combined with a wide spectrum of sounds, sometimes interlocking, sometimes insular, sometimes close by or distant as the mood of the scene is projected. These sounds, trains shunting et cetera, vary in decibels to fit in as a flow-on of a particular emphasis or 'message' to reinforce the setting.

It is a requirement of this play to project an ongoing, almost relentless, momentum, one scene following on another within a very tight time frame. A time slot, at most a few minutes, should occur as a measurement between scenes.

Shoes is not a 'pleasant' play, necessarily so, for Auschwitz and all it represented was an ugly, monstrous, creation of programmed inhumanity.

By probing the layers of characters, inevitably the truth emerges; whatever the circumstances, the complexity of the human condition will forever remain an enigma, a journey unending.

T HE ACTION *throughout takes place in an inmate block in Auschwitz.*
Additional settings (ie. office, lounge, and living room) are created by different,
more focused lighting states. The action is continuous.

The time is December, 1943, Southern Poland, winter. Light rises slowly as we
enter Block A77. Rough narrow wooden bunks, four-tiered, fitted with filthy,
broken straw mattresses are fixed against the rear wall of the block and along the
left wall forming an L-shaped configuration of wooden bunks. At right is the large,
heavy wooden door, partitioned to create two halves. The door gives access to the
yard, acres in size, housing other blocks, and further to the greater expanse of
Auschwitz and its seventeen miles of installations.

An aura permeates the block. It is an aura of degradation and suffering. The
windowless, almost Darwinian, enclave of misery, paradoxical cruelty and living
hell is lit by a few naked light bulbs which now cast an eerie, yellowish, glow,
hardly penetrating the interior corners of this man-made cavern, rooting them in
perpetual darkness.

Besides the tiers of bunks, the only other components of the block are two wooden
crates, centre, which once contained truck batteries, and a third, larger crate, right
centre, near the wooden door. A large, dented, decidedly abused, galvanised iron
bucket stands on the makeshift table. A long soup handle protrudes out of the
mouth of the old bucket. Scattered here and there are squatting seats made from
discarded sacks stuffed with straw on which the inmates sometimes sit to devour
their meagre rations of bread and soup.

The floor of the block is of grey cement, grey as the mood of the interior.

I

Shoes

Perceived in the mind, beyond this block are the hundreds of other similar blocks built in disciplined rows mile after mile, like Lego building blocks covering a vast canvas of soil, seventeen square miles of man-made hell on earth. Some three miles from A77 lies Birkenau, adjoining Auschwitz One, where the trains arrive daily and the ramp selections take place. Birkenau, besides its principal function of operating the gas chambers and the crematoriums, also serves as a quarantine camp, a gypsy camp, a women-and-children camp, and an additional men's camp. Still further on, beyond Birkenau is Auschwitz Three, or Monowitz; the industrial centre with its factories and workshops.

Through grimy train windows, arrivals can see watchtowers, walls, low buildings (the blocks), barbed wire fences, and a long cement ramp teeming with officials involved in the selection process. Huge Alsation hounds, snarling and whining, eager to bite, are held on tight leashes by hard faced SS men shouting brutally: 'Los, los heraus und einreihen!' (Get out and form rows). Motley hundreds spill from the cattle trucks. The rayés (the striped ones) rush forward to collect the luggage and belongings of the new arrivals. The gaunt appearance of the rayés alone seems more frightening than the curses of the SS and the vicious dogs. Emaciated, hollow-cheeked, like medieval statues at the portals of Gothic cathedrals, their dead eyes evoke a symbol of what lies in store.

This scenario builds an atmosphere of despair, of abandonment, of living death, compounded with the smell of unwashed bodies; the mouldy food; the all pervasive corpse stench from the belching smoke from the crematoriums; the cadaveric-tasting water; the general dampness that seems to hang over everything like some immovable fog.

As light grows stronger, we hear the chugging of trains somewhere far off. For a few minutes the audience absorbs this scenario. Then, suddenly, loud sounds of marching feet, voices, barked orders, barking dogs. The door crashes open. A stout, beefy, bull-necked SS corporal stomps in, turns back at the entourage following him.

Shoes

SS CORPORAL (*Barks*) Schnell! Schnell! Schnell! You filthy Jewish crap! Do you think I've got nothing better
to do than get you inside?

*Some ten men, mostly in their early forties, all shaven-headed, shuffle inside.
They are clearly exhausted. Clothed in baggy striped uniforms, worn out boots
and makeshift coats made from discarded sacks – a pitiful protection against the
icy cold – all are shivering. Hollow-cheeked, clearly undernourished, they appear
robotic, barely living humans released from labouring twelve to fifteen hours a day
in the factories of I.G. Farben in Monowitz making synthetic rubber. Some have
on striped caps which they discard with effort as though even such a simple act is
beyond their energy. Some flop down on the sack pouffes, some manage to crawl
into their bunks.*

SS CORPORAL (*Amused*) Look at these Jews. Pathetic! Only Germans know how to work. You lot can only lend
money. You make me sick.

A young blond SS guard enters. The corporal turns to him.

SS CORPORAL (*Testily*) Where's that fat-arsed blockawa?

SS GUARD He's helping that French boy. The one with the
swollen feet.

SS CORPORAL (*Aggressively*) Bloody queers! If Farben factories
didn't need the labour, I would have put this lot
into the ovens myself. Look at this bunch. A little
work and they want to sleep. Can you think what
it must be like to be a factory foreman? God
knows how they manage to produce rubber over
there. We get them over there at six every morning, rain, snow, sunshine, wind. Then we fetch
them like schoolboys to be back here at eight
every night. Fourteen hours of labour, non-stop.
And what do these scum produce? Faulty rubber!

3

Not even good enough to make a tractor tyre, much less a tank tyre.

SS GUARD (*Shrugs*) Maybe if they got more food . . .

SS CORPORAL (*Sarcastic*) To turn Auschwitz into a hotel for Jews. Is that your stupid idea, heh?

SS GUARD (*Defensively*) You cannot work without enough food. Even a machine must have oil, a car gasoline.

SS CORPORAL (*Dismissing the discussion*) Go and find that fat-arsed blockawa and his bag-of-bones lover. (*The guard exits and the corporal turns and walks to the end of the stage and addresses the audience with his thoughts.*) The only reason why I put up with this blockawa and his lover is because he is the best thief in Auschwitz. Whenever I have to search him, he always nods – this pocket for you. You see he works in Canada, the Effektenkammer, where all the belongings of the Jews off the trains are stored. Sometimes I get diamond rings, gold watches, American dollars, English pounds. In turn I smuggle these valuables out. When the war is over I will go to Paraguay a rich man. The Reich doesn't appreciate the work I do here. Do you think it's easy living with this misery every day? Yes, some enjoy being here, but not me. If it weren't for the valuables coming my way, I'd rather go back to the Russian Front. (*Groans of pain come from one of the lower bunks. The corporal struts over to the bunk and addresses the inmates arrogantly*) Stop your noise! This is not a dancehall! (*The inmate's arm flops out of the bunk touching the corporal, who recoils from the contact. He leans forward cautiously and peers at the inmate, whose agonised cries are now stilled)* Gut! Gut! One less to waste Zyklon B on! (*He moves to where two inmates are lying on their pathetic pouffes and shoves them with his boot.)* Hey, wake up! Wake up! (*The two inmates stir, but not fast enough. The corporal reaches over and pulls one inmate up viciously. Gripped by fear of what could happen, the second inmate summons all his energy and gets up quickly.)*

SS CORPORAL   (*Barking*) Du komme hier! Come here! (*The two inmates join the corporal at the bunk*) Take this and put it outside for collection in the morning. (*The two inmates remove the body and carry it outside. As they exit, the young blond SS Guard enters. He gives a very brief glance back at the exiting party*). One less for the gas chamber. (*He smiles broadly*) I should get a bonus for saving all those little blue pellets. (*Laughs loudly*)

SS GUARD   (*Ignoring the remarks*) The blockawa has taken the French boy to the Revier (Infirmary).

SS CORPORAL   (*Looking at his watch, surprised*) Now? But the infirmary is closed.

SS GUARD   No, it was still open.

SS CORPORAL   (*Annoyed*) Damn! Now I will be late for supper. Steak and onions tonight. And potatoes. And sauerkraut – even if there's no port. Maybe some schnapps too. It's Hendel's birthday.

SS GUARD   I will wait. If you agree, I will wait for the blockawa and you can go.

SS CORPORAL A good idea. Do you want me to save you some schnapps for later?

SS GUARD Thank you. That would be nice, Corporal Schmidt. And don't worry. I will handle things here.

SS CORPORAL Very well. Good night.

SS GUARD Good night.

(Corporal Schmidt exits. The guard paces about, bored. The two inmates from the body detail return and very quietly go to their respective bunks. The guard lights a cigarette, takes a few puffs, then thinks better of it and extinguishes it. He glances around guiltily, for smoking is strictly prohibited in the blocks. Some inmates release their suppressed coughs, kept in whilst Schmidt was present. They know that this particular SS guard is not as bad as Schmidt, who is a fanatical Jew-hater. One inmate even finds the courage to speak.)

INMATE *(Leaning out the bunk)* Where's the Kapo? We're hungry. In another four hours we have to be up again for the appel (roll call). *(A second inmate now also voices his opinion)*

SECOND INMATE He gets away with everything. I bet he's busy making some deal or other with the revier staff, (Infirmary staff). *(Approaching voices are heard)*

SS GUARD *(Indicating)* Here they come. *(The Kapo, Hans Brauer, enters followed by his young lover. The Kapo is a brutish, bull-faced man of thirty with a thick neck, with folds at the back of his head like layers of surplus flesh. He looks well fed, almost fat, in sharp contrast to the rest of the inmates. His small, pig-like eyes constantly dart about, suspicious of everyone and every-thing. He is a confirmed hater, but, strangely, has some love in his otherwise brutal and sadistic nature. The*

6

twisted love he pours out on his fifteen-year-old lover, Louie Mausalt, a French Jew. Louie is quite beautiful. He has fine, delicate features, tall and almost graceful – in contrast to Hans Brauer. Although he is thin, undernourished, pale and walks with difficulty, he does not look sickly. Both are wearing striped uniforms and have shaven heads like the other inmates. Tucked behind Hans Brauer's back, in his trousers, is a long, thick, black rubber truncheon. Brauer does not hesitate to use it at every opportunity. Needless to say, the inmates hate him and fear him, but still find the courage to bait him.)

HANS (Scratching himself as though plagued by lice, speaks to guard) We had to wait a long time for the nurse. When she came she gave us nothing. (Louie stands sheepishly silent beside Hans holding on to his sleeve)

INMATE'S VOICE FROM THE BUNKS (Loudly, sarcastic) Cut the crap you stinking Mistkäfer! (dung beetle)

ANOTHER INMATE'S VOICE. Where's the food?

NOW A CHORUS OF COMPLAINTS We're hungry! Get the food! Get the food! Get the food!

SS GUARD (Annoyed, but with an undertone of sympathy) Go fetch food. These men must soon get back to work. (Hans jerks Louie's hand off his sleeve, takes out his truncheon and rushes at the bunks lashing out indiscriminately as he dashes to and fro. The inmates cower and duck.)

HANS (Exploding with anger) Scumbags! Filthy rotten Jews! I hate you all!

7

SS GUARD (*Shouting*) Stop it! (*Hans ignores the command and continues to curse and smash his truncheon against the bunks in an attempt to strike at the cowering inmates. But now noise breaks out as the inmates shout obscenities. The guard rushes forward, grabs hold of the truncheon and shouts*) Give it to me now! Right now! (*Scowling, Hans releases the truncheon. The noise has attracted attention. Two guards followed by a Feldwebel storm inside. The Feldwebel (sergeant) is one Joseph Kramer. A short, stocky, bespectacled, mean and arrogant disciplinarian, a devoted Nazi; but not averse to anything in his favour. The young blond guard stiffens at Kramer's entry. Hans Brauer calms down. The block reverts to total silence. The two new guards position themselves, rifles at the ready. Louie clasps his hands together, moves meekly out the way.*)

KRAMER (*All keyed up*) What's going on here? What's all this noise?

HANS (*Defensively*) These scumbags are shouting for their food.

KRAMER (*Sneeringly*) Ag so! Food, ja. Shouting for food. Pay attention, Juden. Guards wake them up! (*The guards, but not the blond guard, move to the bunks, move up and down, and shout 'Pay attention!' The inmates lean out. Satisfied that he has everyone's attention, Kramer continues menacingly*). Be careful Juden! Be very careful! We Germans tolerate no trouble from Jews! (*Screaming*) Achte deine vorgesetzten! You understand that? You hear that? It means respect your superiors! (*Pause, he struts up and down, hands clasped behind his back, then stands with arms akimbo. Another menacing speech follows.)* The rules are – ruhe im block – you understand – no noise. Any more noise and it's time for the Himmelfahrtblock – ja – you understand what I'm saying – it's time for the crematorium. *(He waits for his words to sink in. Then after a short pause, calls to the two guards)* Komme, let's get away from here.

BLOND SS GUARD   *(Addressing Kramer)* Must I stay?

KRAMER   *(Contemptuously)* Ach, its all of Israel here. No, come with us. *(Kramer, followed by three guards, exits. As he goes, he curses aloud.)* Himmelfahrtblock, ja!

HANS   *(Spitting at Kramer's departure)* Nazi pig!

VOICE FROM THE BUNKS   Hypocrite! You kiss their arses!

ANOTHER VOICE   You stinking Mistkäfer. (dung beetle)

HANS   *(Menacingly)* I'll smash your skull!

A NUMBER OF VOICES   Fetch the food! Fetch the food! We're hungry! We're hungry!

LOUIE   I'm hungry too, Hans. Let me go and fetch the food – please!

HANS   *(Disapprovingly)* You're too slow, Louie, with your sore feet. You sit and wait. I'll go. *(Louie, disappointed, goes over to one of the box chairs and sits down. Hans takes the pail and leaves to fetch the ration of soup and bread.)*

VOICE OF AN IN-MATE IN THE BUNKS   *(Concerned)* The soup will be gone. It's late. The kitchens will be closed.

ANOTHER VOICE The kitchen's like the crematoriums, never shut. There will be soup.

ANOTHER VOICE (*Contemptuously*) Slop, you mean, slop – not soup!

ANOTHER VOICE (*Sarcastic*) Do you want a menu?

ANOTHER VOICE Stop carping and shut up. I want to get some sleep. (*Louie in the meantime has removed his boots. He sits quietly massaging his sore feet for a few moments, then he begins to sing. A soft, tender, melodious voice in a beautiful French accent. The little melody goes something like:*

> I see the face of my Mama
> She is smiling at me
> Through her tears
> Is she thinking of me?
> The moon tonight is soft and white
> My heart is sad.
> Oh, why did you leave me?
> The moon is gone
> And I am alone,
> All alone.
> Please come back some day
> Oh, Mama, Oh Mama,
> I do love you so –

Halfway through his song, one half of the door has opened slightly. There is someone (unseen) listening to Louie's plaintive melody.)

VOICE FROM THE BUNKS Stop singing that crap.

ANOTHER VOICE Leave him alone. He's just a boy.

ANOTHER VOICE It's beautiful. Sing some more.

(Encouraged, Louie proceeds to sing the melody once more. Only now, his voice sounds more hauntingly lonely than before, but still very beautiful. The door now opens wide and a handsome, immaculately uniformed SS officer enters. He is dark, tall and youthful, with a glow of vitality. He wears a full-length leather coat over his pressed, spotless uniform and has on a pair of leather gloves. This is Rudolf Steiner, twenty-eight; sauve, educated – a man with flair, style and sophistication. His panache is incongruous with his military vocation, as he comes from a background of wealth and influence. His rank is that of an SS Unterstürmführer (Second Lieutenant). As he walks nearer, Louie immediately stops his melody. His eyes take in Steiner wearily.)

LOUIE *(Frightened)* I wasn't making a noise – just singing softly.

STEINER *(Pleasantly)* Please continue.

LOUIE *(Hesitantly)* I can't really sing – only pretend.

STEINER *(Smiling)* Pretend then.

LOUIE *(Uncomfortably, nervously)* I just make things up. I've already forgotten the words.

STEINER *(Removing his gloves, gently)* It was about your mother?

LOUIE *(Sadly)* She is dead.

STEINER *(With sympathy)* Here? Did she die here?

LOUIE *(Quietly)* No – Paris. *(A short, uncomfortable silence follows. Steiner is not insensitive to the boy's loss)*

STEINER *(Warmly, steering Louie away from his mother's death)* Ah, Paris. What a beautiful city. Truly a feast for one's eyes and soul.

LOUIE *(Naively, curiously)* You have been there?

STEINER Oh yes, many times.

LOUIE *(Still nervous, unsure what to make of Steiner)* When?

STEINER May I sit? (*By now some heads have cautiously begun to watch the pair from their bunks*)

LOUIE (*With trepidation*) If you wish.

STEINER Now – what is your name? (*Louie does not answer and stares at Steiner with fear and confusion. An SS officer chatting with a Jew?*) Come now, I'm not going to harm you.

LOUIE (*Hesitant, but sensing Steiner's sincerity*) Louie Mausalt.

STEINER (*Realising the situation and Louie's reluctance*) You don't like us Germans?

LOUIE (*Evasively*) I'm very hungry.

STEINER (*Concerned*) No food? Where is the Kapo?

LOUIE (*Protectively*) He's fetching the soup.

STEINER Good. (*Pause*) Well, while we wait for the Kapo to bring the soup, tell me about yourself. (*The light now focuses on Louie and Steiner, fading the bunks into darkness*)

LOUIE (*Suspiciously*) Are you Gestapo?

STEINER (*Reassuringly – laughs*) Do I look like Gestapo?

LOUIE (*Unsure*) But you are a German and I am a Jew. (*Very slight pause*) Why are you here?

STEINER You mean why am I talking with you. Me an SS German officer and you a Jewish inmate?

LOUIE (*Simply*) Yes.

STEINER (*Pleasantly*) Very well, Louie. (*Very slight pause*) May I call you Louie? (*Louie nods approval*). Good. Well, let's see, where do I begin? Why am I here? (*Very slight pause*). I was born in Berlin . . .

LOUIE   (*Interrupting, more confident now*) I was born in Paris. On the seventeenth of November.

STEINER   A scorpio. (*Louie smiles now, nods*). Good. Scorpio is a good sign. My sign is the crab. Cancer.

LOUIE   (*Interested, now more at ease*) Tell me about Berlin.

STEINER   Very well. Berlin is a very beautiful city. Beautiful buildings with parks and trees and flowers and boulevards. A city of culture and elegance and charm and music. Very much like Paris.

LOUIE   (*Engrossed*) Like Paris?

STEINER   Yes, just like Paris. You will like Berlin, Louie. (*Very slight pause*) Do you like music, Louie?

LOUIE   (*Curious*) Are you a composer?

STEINER   (*Amused*) A composer – no. A pianist, yes, but a composer – no.

LOUIE   (*Surprised*) You can play the piano?

STEINER   Yes.

LOUIE   (*Excited*) Tell me about it!

STEINER   My father is the conductor of a very big and important orchestra in Berlin. And my mother a concert pianist. Without sounding opinionated, I play the piano. So you see we are quite a musical family, Louie.

LOUIE   What do you play on your piano?

STEINER   Oh – Chopin mainly, some others . . .

LOUIE   (*Demanding*) But tell me why you are here. You are not like the others. You are different. A

German talking with me a Jew! I cannot understand . . .

STEINER We started on that track, Louie, but we moved away. So all right, let me explain –

LOUIE (*Interrupting*) But why are you SS?

STEINER (*A bit peeved*) Give me a chance to explain.

LOUIE (*Humbly*) Sorry.

STEINER In 1939 I joined the army after completing my studies in law at the University of Berlin. I –

LOUIE (*Interrupting again, confused*) You are a lawyer, not a pianist?

STEINER Yes, a lawyer. A lawyer by profession, a pianist by choice. (*Louie looks puzzled*). What I mean, Louie, is I will make my living practising law some day, and play the piano for relaxation. Do you understand now . . .?

LOUIE (*Losing interest*) Look, I have some numbers on my arm. (*Holds up his arm for Steiner to see*).

STEINER (*Disappointed*) I see. (*Very slight pause. Steiner realises Louie's interest has waned. Moves on*) How long have you been in Auschwitz?

LOUIE Two years. I work at Monowitz with the others in the rubber factory. But Hans, the Kapo, he works in Canada, the Effektenkamer, the Warehouse. He is lucky.

STEINER (*Gently*) What about your family, your parents? Do you have brothers and sisters?

LOUIE (*Hopelessly, sadly*) All gassed. All gone. The soldiers took us to Drancy first and then later put us on the trains. On the ramp, the selection, I was the only one told not to get into the trucks going to the showers. Later the other prisoners told me the showers were the gas chambers.

STEINER (*Taking pity*) Would you like to move to another part of the camp? The vegetable and flower gardens of the Kommandant? There are horses and other animals there too. Perhaps you would like that?

LOUIE (*Rubbing his stomach*) I get so hungry.

STEINER Well at the Kommandant's area there is plenty of food. Fresh vegetables. Even meat.

LOUIE (*Interest re-kindled*) Is there chicken?

STEINER Plenty. Hundreds.

LOUIE (*Downcast*) But I am a Jew. I will get nothing.

STEINER It does not matter. All the Kommandant's workers get extra rations.

LOUIE I work on a machine. It makes black sticky stuff to go into rubber. I don't know anything about gardens or vegetables.

STEINER The other workers will teach you. You have only to learn.

LOUIE I like work, but my feet get sore and tired from standing all day. The Kapo in charge will not let anybody sit. We have to stand all day for fifteen hours. The only time I can leave my machine is to go and pass water. Look how my feet are swollen. (*Holds up one foot for Steiner to see. Steiner looks, but does not comment.*)

STEINER Your work is helping to win the war,

Louie. Look at it that way. (*He retracts*) That was a stupid thing to say. I apologise.

LOUIE (*Simply, then yearningly*) I hate war. Only music is good. And Paris. And warm bread. And milk. Maybe some cheese. And fruit. And chicken and – and flowers . . .(*Louie puts his boots back on*).

STEINER Would you like to come to Berlin after the war is over?

LOUIE (*Lighting up*) Berlin!

STEINER (*Expansively*) You can take singing lessons. I know many good tutors. It will be a wonderful opportunity for you. You can be very happy. Berlin is a place for culture and the arts. Would you like that?

LOUIE (*Unsure*) I don't know. I am a Jew. Jews are only meant to die and suffer. No, I will never get to Berlin.

STEINER But I will help you – I want to help you.

LOUIE Why?

STEINER Because you remind me very much of someone I knew.

LOUIE Who?

STEINER It's a long story.

LOUIE Tell me. (*Steiner looks at the watch on his wrist.*)

STEINER I must leave. We will talk again.

LOUIE Tomorrow?

STEINER (*Getting up*) Perhaps. (*As Steiner rises, Hans enters carrying the pail of soup. He places the pail on the*

16

wooden crate. His eyes dart towards Steiner. Full of suspicion, he watches Steiner and Louie.)

LOUIE When can I go to work in the Kommandant's vegetable garden?

STEINER I will have to arrange it through the proper channels first. Tomorrow I will speak with my superior officer.

LOUIE (*Getting up*) Look at my feet. I cannot work in the factory any more. (*Light now brightens*)

STEINER (*Sympathetically*) I understand. Leave it with me. Good night. (*He looks into the soup pail briefly and into Hans' face, but Hans avoids eye contact*) Is this good? (*He puts on his gloves*)

HANS (*Forcing eye contact and a phoney smile*) Yes, Herr Steiner.

STEINER Good, I'm pleased to hear it. (*Steiner exits*)

HANS (*As the door shuts*) Good pig slop! (*Louie approaches Hans. The inmates begin to scramble from their bunks and come forward for their soup ration. They each carry a tin bowl.*)

LOUIE Do you know him?

HANS (*Full of suspicion*) What does he want with you, huh? What?

LOUIE (*Hurt*) I asked if you know him. (*The inmates shove their bowls at Hans. He proceeds to ladle out the soup, being very careful not to spill a drop*)

HANS Yes, I know him. He comes into the warehouse sometimes. This block is under his command, but he leaves the dirty work to Kramer. Be careful of him. (*Carries on ladling soup*)

LOUIE   He spoke nicely to me. (*Hans stiffens*)

HANS   (*Angrily*) Are you mad?! (*Relaxes*) You canary brain.

LOUIE   We spoke about music and Berlin.

HANS   (*About to explode*) What kind of shit is that?! Music and Berlin! Are you going soft in the head?

LOUIE   Not now. After the war is over. He wants me to go to Berlin.

HANS   (*Bursts out laughing*) What a shithead you are!

INMATE   You're spilling soup! (*Hans turns on him, shoving him away, spilling yet more soup*)

INMATES IN   The soup is being wasted!
CHORUS, ANGRY

HANS   (*Shouting back*) All right! It's my share. Get away!

LOUIE   You're making fun of me. It's true, the war will end.

HANS   (*Finds it very amusing*) Himmel, you are a funny kid. The war is over long ago. That SS pig is putting a lot of shit into your head. Get your bowl and get some soup. Maybe the food will fix your brains. (*Louie makes a face, goes to his bunk to collect his bowl. But he cannot find it, searches.*)

FEISTY INMATE   I don't want your pig slop! Where's the bread ration? (*Hans ignores him. Inmate not to be fobbed off*) I reckon you traded it for something for yourself again. You pig!

HANS   (*Threateningly*) Get away! (*An inmate takes the feisty inmate by the sleeve, motioning him away before Hans explodes with his truncheon*).

ANOTHER FEISTY INMATE Stir the soup, goddammit! (*Hans gives the ladle a good swirl, careful not to go too deep so that the best part, the thick vegetables, will be left for him.*)

ANOTHER INMATE No sausage? No margarine? Where's the bread? I don't want this pig swill turnip soup. It's nothing but pig piss!

HANS (*Shrugs it off*) Please yourself. More to share.

INMATE (*Spits*) Pig!

HANS (*Threateningly*) Watch it! Any more crap from you and your head will come off! (*He pulls out the truncheon from his back trousers and puts it alongside the soup bucket*)

INMATE (*Walking away*) Choke, you bastard!

HANS (*Shouting at the bunks. Some inmates have not come for their rations*) Last call for soup! After this, no more. You hear? No more! (*Louie comes to Hans and hands him his bowl. Hans snatches it, digs deep down into the bucket, fills Louie's bowl with thick soup. Louie smiles appreciatively. Hans smiles and gives him a wink. Louie goes over to his box chair, sits down, proceeds to sip his soup from the bowl, as no spoons are permitted. Hans shouts again: Last call for soup! An inmate goes over to one of the bunks where the occupant has not reponded to Han's call. He shakes the man. No response.*)

INMATE (*Calling to Hans*) Zarnick is dead! (*Louie stops eating, looks at the inmate*)

A VOICE FROM THE SHADOW OF THE BUNKS I want his share. (*Louie carries on eating*)

19

ANOTHER VOICE No, you must share. (*An inmate clambers out of his bunk, rushes over to Hans with his tin bowl, shoves it at Hans*)

INMATE I was first.

HANS Get away! (*The inmate raises his bowl, crashes it down on Hans' head. Hans shoots out a huge hand into the man's face and shoves him away.*) Stupid Jew! From tomorrow no more holzhof (the easy life) for you. At aufstehen (roll call) I put you on report – the Nacht and Nebel – the salt mines for you!

INMATE (*Defiantly as he returns to his bunk*) Go ahead! The salt mines don't scare me. Nothing scares me in this hell anymore.

HANS (*Smirks*) Big mouth! Ja, all Jews have big mouths till they get into the gas chambers. Then cries, then tears.

INMATE NEXT TO THE BODY. (*Speaks to Hans specifically*) What about Zarnick?

HANS (*Indifferent*) So? He's kaput. Leave him till morning. You take him outside now, you're dead. It's curfew time. The dogs will get you. He won't stink till morning. (*Pause in action, then – half dead inmate approaches Hans with his soup bowl. His voice is weak.*)

INMATE More soup? (*Hans bursts out laughing, holding on to his sides, a minute of loud laughter.*)

HANS (*Recovering. Now full of sarcasm.*) Is there more? (*Mimics the inmate*) More soup? (*Laughs again*). Ja, there is. What would you like with it? Chocolate cake with walnuts, maybe? Potatoes? Meat with onions? Ice cream? Huh? Tell me! (*The inmate is too weak to argue or confront Hans and shuffles off.*)

CHORUS OF CATCALLS FROM THE BUNKS Du Mistkäfer! (dung beetle)

HANS (*Retaliates, shouts*) Jewish swine!

The one half of the door opens, a guard holding a torch in his hand, looks in. 'Ruhe im block' (Quiet in block) he warns, then adds, 'Lights off soon. Finish your food.' The door shuts.

HANS (*Making an 'up yours' sign at the door*) German dog!

CHORUS FROM SOME INMATES Hypocrite! Nazi arselicker!

HANS (*Ignores their taunting. Pours soup into a much bigger bowl. Satisfies himself the bucket is empty, moves to join Louie. Light now changes. Bunks fall into darkness. Light focuses on Hans and Louie sitting opposite each other. Louie has finished his soup, watches Hans slurp his soup noisely.*) Ahh . . .

LOUIE (*Plaintively*) I'm still hungry. My stomach is sore. (*Hans glances over his shoulder. Satisfied that everyone else is now asleep, he furtively removes a rolled up, dirty, soiled cloth from his coat pocket. He unravels the cloth. Gingerly he removes a chunk of sausage. Louie's face lights up.*)

HANS (*Lowering his voice, not to be overheard*) For you, my little angel.

LOUIE (*Takes the piece of sausage, devours it greedily. Between mouthfuls . . .*) Hmmm . . . Hmmm . . . Nice . . . So nice . . .

HANS   (*Puts down his bowl, wipes his mouth on his sleeve, and begins to stroke Louie's arm*) Just for you, my little angel. Just for you.

LOUIE   (*Shoving his arm off, sensing his motive*) Not tonight. I'm tired.

HANS   (*Sucking up, sugary, almost pleading, but not quite assertive*) Just a few kisses.

LOUIE   (*Adamantly but petulantly*) No.

HANS   (*Not to be put off, now connives*) Would you like some chicken?

LOUIE   (*Thrilled*) Chicken! Real chicken?

HANS   (*Back to stroking, Louie's leg now*) Tomorrow. To-morrow I bring you real chicken. As much as you can eat. (*Pause*) Now what about a little feel, heh?

LOUIE   (*Softening*) But no lovemaking. You can only feel. Promise?

HANS   (*Eagerly*) Yes, I promise. (*He takes Louie in his arms, embracing him, smothering him with kisses. The focus of light slowly fades, darkness envelops.*)

It is early morning. Light rises out from the darkness. Music drifts into the block – 'Wien, wien, nur du allein.' The door crashes open. Two guards enter. Both are wearing heavy overcoats as protection against the cold. The inmates, all in their bunks, begin to stir restlessly.

FIRST GUARD   (*Rubbing his hands together*) This five a.m. shift is the worst in winter.

SECOND GUARD   Ja, but what can we do? Befehl ist befehl ('an order is an order'). (*Hans climbs from his bunk. Rubs the sleep out of his eyes*)

HANS (*Puzzled*) What is going on? What's happening? Are we to start our shift an hour earlier now?

FIRST GUARD Are you the Kapo for this block?

HANS (*Worried*) Yes – yes.

FIRST GUARD Routine inspection.

HANS (*Relieved*) Oh.

SECOND GUARD (*Amused*) He thought we'd come to collect them for the gas – ja. (*Both guards laugh. All the inmates are awake now and are leaning out of their bunks waiting for the next episode to occur. They do not wait long. Kramer struts in like a cocky rooster. He carries a riding crop which he taps against his leg.*)

KRAMER (*Struts up and down barking an order*) Los, los, heraus und einreihen! (Get out and form rows.) (*The inmates begin to leave their bunks. Louie does not stir, he sleeps through the commotion. Neither does Zarnick, for he is dead. The pace of the inmates vacating their bunks is not fast enough for Kramer. He waves at the guards to get them moving faster. He barks louder, more menacingly, slapping the riding crop hard now against his leg.*) Raus! Raus! Alles raus! Schnell! Schnell! Befehl ist befehl! Raus, raus, und einreihen! (*The two guards shove the inmates into a straight line. To impress Kramer, Hans wields his truncheon menacingly but does not strike anyone. Kramer notices the two inmates still in their bunks. One guard hauls the sleepy Louie from his bunk. The other guard tries to revive Zarnick.*)

GUARD (*Calls to Kramer*) This man is dead.

KRAMER (*Unperturbed*) Gut. Eine minder vir Birkenau.

(One less for Birkenau – the crematorium.) (*The guard returns to stand next to Kramer, who adds, smirking*) Eine minder Juden. (One less Jew.) (*The guard smiles broadly. Kramer struts up and down inspecting the inmates like a butcher in a slaughterhouse examining cattle. An exhausted inmate collapses at Kramer's feet. Kramer jumps back, fearful of making contact. He then shoves the prostrate inmate with his foot.*) Raus! Raus! *He barks.* (*The man does not move. It is obvious now that he is dead. Kramer motions to the guards to remove the body. They drag the body to one side. Satisfied that the inmates now have his attention, he stands in front of them like a schoolmaster.*) Our Kommandant will be doing inspection tomorrow. Halte dich sauber! (Keep clean) You understand? (*The inmates nod*) Gut, gut. (*He singles out Louie*) You, you stay behind. A cleaning squad is coming to fumigate. You must help turn the mattresses over. Understood? (*Louie nods*). The rest of you, get to work. (*Kramer turns to the guards*) Let them take the bodies out. (*The guards indicate to the inmates to remove the two dead. The inmates carry the bodies out.*) Gut. Now you all get out! (*The block clears with only Louie now remaining.*)

LOUIE (*To himself*) What am I going to do? I cannot turn the mattresses because my feet hurt. I shall do nothing until the fumigators arrive. (*The door opens and who should walk in but Hans. Louie looks at him surprised*) Hans!

HANS (*Putting a finger against his lips*) SSSSSSSHHHHH –

LOUIE (*Curious*) How does a Kapo get away? Are you in trouble?

HANS (*Glancing about anxiously*) No, no trouble. Kramer sent me on an errand. I managed to sneak away for a few minutes by bribing the guard with a gold pen I stole out of the warehouse. It belonged to a Jewish doctor. He won't be writing any more. Puff – just smoke now!

LOUIE (*Worried*) You'd better go back now to the warehouse, the fumigators are coming.

HANS Yes, yes, I'm going back, but I want to talk with you first.

LOUIE (*Puzzled*) With me? Why?

HANS I don't like the way that SS was talking to you last night. You must stay away from him.

LOUIE (*Annoyed*) How can I? He is SS. The SS are God here, they can do anything they like. Must I say to him – go away and leave me alone? Do you know what he can do to me? He can send me straight to the gas chambers. (*Hans rushes over to Louie and holds him in a bear hug.*)

HANS (*Tenderly*) I love you my little angel. I love you. I love you. (*Louie wriggles free*)

LOUIE I'm tired and my feet are sore. You'd better go. Soon they will be looking for you.

HANS (*Upset at the rejection*) I know what he wants with you!

LOUIE So? What?

HANS (*Firmly*) You must not encourage him. When he

comes to talk with you, pretend that you are asleep!

LOUIE   (*Amazed*) Pretend? Pretend with the SS? Are you mad?

HANS   (*Desperately, pleading now*) Please, my little angel – please! I'll bring you chicken, real chicken, I promise. Please, my little angel. You're all I have in this stinking place.

LOUIE   (*Playing up*) He won't be the first. I was raped many times by the SS. They took me away from Drancy one night to Sante prison. All night they got on top of me, one by one, until the blood made them stop.

HANS   (*Agonising, wringing his hands*) Stop it! Oh God, stop it!

LOUIE   (*Not averse now to a brutal enjoyment of his hold on Hans*) One more SS. So – it doesn't matter. Besides he said he was going to help me get work at the Kommandant's house where I will get chicken, fruit, all kinds of nice things. And there are animals too. Maybe I can get a horse and I'll ride away from this place and go back to Paris. Maybe he will take me to Berlin. All kinds of things he can do for me. The SS can do anything they want. They are God. (*Hans falls on his knees in front of Louie, takes his hands in his*)

HANS   (*Weeping*) No! No! No! No! Please, my little angel! I'll get you anything you want. A gold watch. You like that – a gold watch? Hey, my little darling, my little sweetheart, my little angel. Anything, anything, you want. Just say you're mine Louie. Please – please – please! (*Voices are heard. Footsteps approaching. Louie abruptly pulls his hands free. Hans gets up quickly, goes over to the door, listens, cautiously peeps out. Finding it's still all clear, quickly goes out*)

LOUIE   (*To himself dreaming*) Maybe the Kommandant will send me back to Paris . . . (*The door opens, two inmates enter. Both have large cylinders with long hoses attached to their backs. This is the fumigation squad detailed by Kramer to fumigate the block*)

FIRST INMATE TO   You start that end. I'll start here. Then we meet
SECOND INMATE   in the middle. (*Second inmate nods. They get to work preparing their equipment.*)

LOUIE   You must turn the mattresses first.

FIRST INMATE   Who are you – the Kommandant? (*They laugh*)

SECOND INMATE   We'd spray you before we waste this stuff on the mattresses. We're not stinking Jews. We're Gentiles.

LOUIE   (*Surprised*) Gentiles? Then why are you here?

SECOND INMATE   Is it your business?

FIRST INMATE   Okay. We'll tell you because you're just a stupid looking French kid.

LOUIE   (*Offended*) I'm not stupid!

SECOND INMATE   Calm down. We're not the Gestapo. What my partner wanted to tell you is we're traders, see? We were selling meat. Meat that was meant for the Wehrmacht, the Army. They caught us one night with a lot of meat hidden in the hay on the back of our truck. So that's why we are here. Now that you know, leave us alone to fumigate.

LOUIE Does the stuff stink?

FIRST INMATE Less than the crematoriums.

SECOND INMATE (*Laughs*) For a frog eater you want to know a lot. Don't you know that in Auschwitz asking too many questions will put you into the ovens?

FIRST INMATE Why aren't you working?

LOUIE Because I have to help turn the mattresses. (*The inmates burst out laughing*)

FIRST INMATE (*After a good laugh*) We don't turn any goddamed mattresses for Jews. We spray, that's enough.

LOUIE (*Confused*) But we're all together. Look at your heads. They are shaved like mine. And your clothes. Striped like mine. Why are we different then, even if I am a Jew? (*The inmates laugh again. No work is getting done*)

SECOND INMATE We're different because it's all the fault of you Jews that the Germans built these goddamed places. If it weren't for you Jews, there wouldn't have been a need for Auschwitz. You Jews caused this goddammed war because you were greedy and took over everything. Now the Nazis are getting their own back by putting you all in the ovens.

LOUIE (*Plaintively*) But my father was a carpenter and my mother a seamstress. We were not rich. We were very poor. We stole nothing from the Germans.

FIRST INMATE Never mind. We're not here to teach you politics. Go and sit in the corner over there so that we can get on with our work.

SECOND INMATE   You should be in the children's camp. This block is for men only.

LOUIE   (*Defensively*) Leave me alone.

FIRST INMATE   (*Aggressively*) Don't get cheeky with us! We'll . . . (*His words tail off as suddenly the door opens and Steiner appears. The two inmates quickly start preparing their equipment again. Louie smiles at Steiner's appearance, much to the bafflement of the two fumigators.*)

STEINER   (*Addressing the two fumigators*) What are you doing here?

FIRST INMATE   (*Shaky voice*) Spraying for lice, Herr Oberscharführer.(Boss)

STEINER   (*Forcefully*) Get out! You can come back later! (*The two inmates pick up their equipment and promptly leave*)

LOUIE   They won't turn the mattresses.

STEINER   Never mind. Later I'll send a corporal with them to supervise.

LOUIE   We don't have lice in this block. Why must they spray?

STEINER   Regulations. If we do not spray the risk of typhus increases.

LOUIE   (*Tries to pronounce the word*) T − I − E − S − U − S. What is that?

STEINER   A very bad disease. Terrible.

LOUIE   Will I get it?

STEINER   Not if you keep yourself clean.

LOUIE   There isn't enough soap. Can you get me some soap?

STEINER I'll try. (*Pause*)

LOUIE Hans does not want me to talk with you.

STEINER (*Puzzled*) Oh? And who is Hans?

LOUIE The Kapo. You know, that man who was serving the soup last night. He said I must be careful of you.

STEINER Interesting. Why? (*Louie goes over to sit on one of the box chairs centre. Steiner follows and sits on the box chair opposite him.*)

LOUIE He's jealous. He thinks you want me. Do you?

STEINER Want you?

LOUIE Make love with me.

STEINER This Hans has quite an imagination.

LOUIE (*Hurt*) You don't want to take me? We are alone. You can do it now if you want to. (*A fairly long pause*).

STEINER (*With emotion*) I don't know. I don't really know . . .

LOUIE (*Pouting*) Don't you like me? Am I too skinny for you?

STEINER (*Gently*) I like you, Louie. Yes, I like you, Louie.

LOUIE (*Sadly*) Then why don't you want me? You don't have to give me chicken or take me to Berlin. You were so kind to me. Not like Hans. Hans is just like an animal. He always just takes me. He doesn't really care for me. But before you, he was all I had. He protects me against the others. They all want me. But for you I'm willing.

(*A fairly long pause. Steiner is grappling with the situation. Grappling within*

himself. Grappling with emotions that are pouring through his blood. Confused . . .
this boy . . . memories . . .)

STEINER *(Patiently)* You remind me very much of someone who was very dear to me. It's difficult for me to explain how I feel about you, Louie. I need time.

LOUIE *(Hurt)* Is it because I am a Jew and you are a German?

STEINER No, Louie, no. It has nothing to do with whether you are Jewish and me German. It's something from my past. A long story. It's hard for me, Louie. Please understand.

LOUIE Please tell me.

STEINER Some other time, Louie.

LOUIE *(Pleading)* Please, just a little. Nobody tells me anything. They all treat me like I'm just a child. A plaything. But I can understand. Talk to me. Please. Please tell me. Tell me so that I can understand too. I want to understand. I want to understand why you, an SS officer, talks to me so kindly. See, I'm not just a child. A fool whose body gets used like a doll. I have a mind too . . . *(Pause)*

STEINER *(Thoughtfully)* It was a long time ago . . .

LOUIE It doesn't matter. I want to hear.

STEINER *(Painfully, recalling)* There was this boy. He was very much like you. When I saw you for the first time, I almost mistook you for him. It was as though he had suddenly come back to life. But I kept my feelings from showing. For a moment I believed I was dreaming, but then I realised, no, no, it wasn't a dream. I was in Auschwitz. You were a prisoner and I was SS. I put it out of my mind, but my true feelings were too strong. I had to talk with you. I had to face what I felt. I . . . (*he stops*)

LOUIE (*Engrossed*) Yes, tell me more. (*Very slight pause*)

STEINER It happened a long time ago.

LOUIE (*Gently, but insistently*) Please!

STEINER (*More to audience, speaking slowly, Louie listens attentively*) It was summer in Berlin. It was a beautiful summer. Everything was so green, so lush. Everybody was feeling good. Germany was turning around economically. The shops were beginning to stock up with all kinds of food. Many jobs were available. Life was good. I was fifteen years old. An only child. My parents were comfortably off. We had a nice house in a good neighbourhood and they were very good to me. They bought me a bicycle for my birthday. I was very proud of it and rode it everywhere. But although I had a good life, I was very lonely. I wished I had a friend. Many times I would cycle into the countryside and sit by myself in the fields for hours and daydream that I had a friend. One day, coming home from school, I saw a large truck parked opposite our house. I was curious and went to see what was going on. I discovered that we were going to have new neighbours because the men from the truck were carrying in furniture. I was very happy because the house had been standing empty for a very long time.

Whilst I was standing there watching the men offload the furniture, a young boy of my own age came out the house. He smiled at me and came over to talk to me. He introduced himself as Fritz Gruber. We liked one another immediately. He invited me inside and introduced me to his mother. She gave us lemonade and cake. Then a little later his father came. A doctor. The parents were delighted when I told them I lived across the way from their newly acquired house. For you see, Fritz, like me, was an only child and lonely too. We became inseparable friends. We did everything together. We were like brothers, only we never fought or even argued. It was as though our souls were as one. So many times I slept at his house and he at mine. Both our parents were so happy with our friendship. Soon our two families became very good friends too because of our friendship. Even in school we sat next to each other and spent all our free time at school in each other's company. So much so, that our teachers complained to our parents that our relationship was unhealthy. But both our parents would hear nothing of it. Our friendship was too strong. Nothing, nothing, could be said by anybody against either of us. Everything we did, we did together. Camping, fishing, hiking, listening to music, going to concerts, to the cinema, cycling, shopping for presents, everything. Then one day we were lying together in the grass on a hill overlooking a beautiful lake. It was a gorgeous day, full of summer sun, and there were flowers everywhere, their scent drifting in the breeze, and the trees were full of birds chirping and singing. It was so idyllic that it could have been a dream. We lay back enjoying the sunshine. It was then Fritz turned to me and asked whether I loved him. I said, yes of course. He leant over me and kissed me. Kissed me on the mouth. It was strange. I had never been kissed on the mouth before. He kissed me again. Longer this time. It tasted sweet and I enjoyed it. Soon he kept on kissing me and then he stopped and asked me whether I knew about love. I was confused. I said yes, I knew about love. My father and mother loved me. No, he said, not that kind of love. The love that he had for me was different. So I said I didn't understand. Then he patiently said he would show me all about it. He unbuttoned my trousers and made love to me in many different ways. I did not object. I was a virgin and innocent. I loved him and was glad it gave him so much pleasure. After some months I began to enjoy his lovemaking and soon I became converted and we became lovers. I felt, and he felt it too, that our parents suspected that we were odd, holding hands so many times, but neither of them ever said anything because they could see how happy we were. (*Very slight pause*) Then one day, it was a holiday and the school was closed, Fritz suggested we go for a picnic up in the hills outside Berlin near a small lake. The summer was past now and it was winter. I said no, no it was too cold for a picnic, but he insisted. He said the long cycle ride to reach the place would be good exercise. So I relented. Our parents packed a delicious lunch and on the way there I told Fritz that I had stolen a bottle of wine from my father's cellar. He was delighted. Many hours later we reached our destination. By the time we sat down to enjoy our lunch, we were quite exhausted from the long cycle ride. We were too tired even to make love. Then I remembered the bottle of wine. Soon we finished it and a few minutes later felt quite tipsy, even a little drunk. Then Fritz started acting the fool. He went down to the small lake and started taking his clothes off. I asked him what he was doing and he replied that he was going for a swim. I shouted to him. 'Are you mad?! The water is ice cold!' But he took no notice of me. No, he replied, the cold water would clear his head. I got up and went down to plead with him. Stubbornly he waded in and began to swim. When he reached the halfway point, in the middle of the lake, he suddenly began to shout that he had developed a cramp. He threw his arms in the air and shouted to me to save him. He went down under the water and then came up again. His shouts were growing weaker. I began to panic. I jerked my clothes off and began to wade into the water. It was ice cold. I grew scared, terribly frightened. My limbs suddenly felt numb. I couldn't move. I began to cry. I saw Fritz go under and come up and then slowly go under again. The water seemed to swallow him up. I just stood there in the icy water and watched him drown. I must have stood there for hours because the sunlight had long since gone and the birds had stopped singing and I felt terribly, terribly alone. I forced myself out of the water. There was no feeling in my body. It was as though I had become a block of ice. With great effort I put on my clothes. I was too scared to go home. I didn't know what to do. Towards midnight, after agonising over what to do, I reached my house and quietly sneaked up into my room. Sometime later I heard my door open slightly and knew it was my father checking up to see whether I was in bed. That night I lay awake all night with my heart beating wildly. In the morning Fritz's parents came knocking on our door to find out if Fritz had spent the night in our house. My father answered the door and told them no. Then he got me out of bed. I went downstairs with him into our living room. No, I lied, I had not been with Fritz for the past few hours. But that's strange, they said, you were on a picnic together. Yes, I lied, we had cycled back together but halfway back Fritz said he had forgotten his watch at the picnic site and had gone back to fetch it. 'Why did I not go back with him?' his father asked, especially since we were such very close friends. I thought quickly and lied that I had an upset stomach from drinking wine. I had to admit in front of my father and Fritz's parents that I had stolen a bottle of my father's wine. But I was not admonished by my father for it, nor by Fritz's parents either. There was something far more serious to worry about. Where was Fritz? Soon the police were notified and together with the police we drove out to the lake, my father and mother and the father and mother of Fritz. His bicycle was still there. The empty bottle of wine was still there. The wrappings from our picnic lunch were still there. But no Fritz. I was the only one who knew. Inside I felt dead. Fear of discovery ate into me like a cancer. For many days, over many hours, on innumerable occasions, the police questioned me, but I stuck to my story. Then they dragged the lake and found his body. Still I stuck to my story. He must have gone for a swim after finding his watch, I said. The police were suspicious but they could prove nothing. Luckily Fritz was found with his watch on, so it seemed a reasonable explanation. As for Fritz's parents, they believed my story and so did my parents. The funeral was terrible for me. I stood at the graveside watching the black coffin containing my friend, my lover's body, go into the mouth of eternity. My tears covered the guilt tearing my heart apart. Afterwards anger filled me, flowed through my blood like a river of fire. I turned to the Hitler Youth. I filled my brain with studies of the law. Then salvation came my way when Hitler proclaimed Germany was at war. I joined the army at the first opportunity. I volunteered for the Einsatzgruppen, the killing squads, to help my anger and went into Russia. Then they, my

superiors, felt I was cracking up, taking my work
too seriously. I needed a break. No, I insisted.
But they won in the end and sent me here. (*Pause*)
So that's the story. The story of Rudolf Steiner.
More I do not wish to tell. (*A fairly long pause*).

LOUIE   You see Fritz in me?

STEINER   Yes.

LOUIE   You loved him very much?

STEINER   Yes, very much.

LOUIE   Can you love me so much?

STEINER   Perhaps.

LOUIE   Hold me.

*Steiner and Louie rise. Steiner holds Louie close. The light fades into darkness.
When light rises it focuses on centre stage bathing a desk on which is a telephone,
some documents in files in a neat pile, a filing cabinet behind the desk as well as
a swivel chair and two visitors' chairs in front of the desk. An enormous blow-up
photograph of Hitler attached to a frame forms a wall now between the office and
the bunks which are in darkness. A channel of light runs from the office to the door
behind which now (unseen) is a reception area manned by an SS corporal. The office
is that of Rudolf Hoess, Kommandant of Auschwitz. For a minute the stage is
bare, then Hoess enters. He is of medium height, middle-aged, balding, somewhat
corpulent, and wears glasses. Nothing really distinguishes the man. He could well
pass for a grocer, a clerk, a schoolteacher. His uniform looks crisp, well tailored and
new. He carries a stack of files which he places on his desk. Sitting down in his
swivel chair he opens a drawer and removes a pack of cigarettes and a box of
matches. Hoess is a chain smoker and throughout this scene he lights up one cigarette
after another, using the butt of one cigarette to light the next. He begins to examine
the documents in one of the files. The corporal on duty enters and Hoess looks up
from his file.*

DUTY CORPORAL (*Stiffly*) Hauptsturmführer (Captain) Kleinsmidt wishes to see you Herr Hoess.

HOESS Very well, show him in. (*The duty corporal returns to the door. We hear him say. 'The Kommandant will see you. Please go inside.' Kleinsmidt enters, closes the door behind him. He is carrying a package, gift wrapped. He marches up to Hoess, salutes, places the gift-wrapped package on the desk and removes his cap. Kleinsmidt is fortyish, tall, straight backed, rather handsome with strong features, all heel clicking, all soldier, totally the higher disciplined, totally committed, SS Officer.*)

KLEINSMIDT Thank you for seeing me, Herr Kommandant. I realise that you are inundated with work. But I wished to bring a small present for Emmi's birthday.

HOESS (*Warmly*) Thank you Werner. Come, sit down for a few minutes. So you have time?

KLEINSMIDT Yes – a few minutes. So much to do, it's becoming hard to find time. (*Shrugs*) But still, duty comes before finding complaints.

HOESS (*Taking the package and placing it in a drawer*) Having three daughters means so many birthdays. Frau Hoess is expecting you to join us tommorrow evening. We're having a small party for Emmi. As always, Frau Hoess is preparing a veritable feast for the occasion. Salmon, roast lamb, chicken, beef, pork, even caviar, real Bolshevik, and champagne, French. And of course, salads, really good tomatoes and cucumbers straight from our own hothouse.

KLEINSMIDT (*Pleased*) I look forward to it. (*Begins to put his cap back on*). Duty calls.

HOESS (*Reaching for a file*) One more minute. There is something I wish to share with you. (*Kleinsmidt puts his cap back on his lap.*)

KLEINSMIDT Very well. (*Hoess opens the file.*)

HOESS (*Beaming*) The latest statistics. Our targets for the month of November have all been accomplished. We are well ahead of the other camps. France is practically swept clean. Pity, though, that there are no funds for a second Katowice – Krakow, line. Just think of it, we could double our Sonderbehandlung and Labour Utilization programme for nineteen forty-four. The Reichsführer will not only dance, he will sing. Think of it, Werner. (*Enthused*) Just think what it will mean to our promotion!

KLEINSMIDT (*Considering*) Yes, it would be nice. But at the moment we cannot handle the numbers already coming in from the East. No sooner do we process fifty thousand a week, than more thousands get off the trains. We need more resources. More ovens. Twenty-four hours a day is not sufficient, not the answer. Berlin must give us additional facilities.

HOESS (*Hearing, but not hearing*) It's really a question of logistics – more ovens would not solve our problems. It's all a question of shortage of trucks. If there were more trucks available, then the numbers coming in could be spaced out more efficiently. Instead, all arrive at the same time.

Believe me, my dear Werner, I sympathise with you. When I go to the ramp and see all those Jews piling out of the box cars, it makes my teeth ache. (*Pause*)

KLEINSMIDT (*Lifting his cap*) With respect, Herr Kommandant, but I must go. (*He looks at his wristwatch*) My men are waiting for me. We are to execute some Polish Jews who attempted an escape.

HOESS Very well. (*Kleinsmidt rises, puts on his cap, clicks his heels and salutes, then exits. Hoess coughs. Complains, 'Ag what a filthy habit', then lights up another cigarette. He closes his file, chooses another. The door opens and the duty corporal enters.*)

DUTY CORPORAL (*Respectfully*) Excuse me, Herr Kommandant. Did you wish to see Feldwebel Kramer? (*Hoess nods*)

Before the duty corporal can grant permission for Kramer to enter, he struts in aggressively. The duty corporal shakes his head at this ill-mannered intrusion and closes the door. Kramer salutes.

KRAMER (*Faking a smile, slimy*) You wish to see me, Herr Kommandant?

HOESS (*Businesslike*) Yes. Sit down. (*Kramer removes his cap, sits stiffly*).

KRAMER (*Tense*) Herr Kommandant?

HOESS (*Very tactfully*) What do you know about Second Lieutenant Steiner?

KRAMER (*Not fully understanding the question*) I work under his command, Herr Hoess – (*He corrects himself*) Herr Kommandant.

HOESS (*With an edge of impatience*) I mean as a person.

(*Then more patiently*) How do you and your men find him as a person? Friendly, cold, aloof, stubborn – what? Surely, you have an opinion?

KRAMER (*Unsure of his ground*) Well . . . Herr Kommandant . . . He is a rather strange, a rather complex officer, if I may put it that way. He mixes with no one. Retires to his quarters and reads. All his books are above me. Philosophy. Art. Music. That kind of thing. (*Pause*)

HOESS (*Bluntly*) Is he soft? (*Kramer shifts uneasily on his chair. He is caught in a conundrum. Steiner is his superior. He is aware that Steiner pulls weight in Berlin through family connections as high as the Führer. This has been common gossip even before Steiner's arrival at the camp from the Russian front*)

KRAMER (*Fencing*) Perhaps. Sometimes he doesn't like what he has to do.

HOESS (*Firmly*)Like?

KRAMER The inmates being taken care of.

HOESS (*Rubbing his chin*) The showers?

KRAMER Yes.

HOESS (*Probing*) Anything else? (*A fairly long pause whilst Kramer thinks.*)

KRAMER (*Loosening up a bit*) He never watches punishment meted out. Gives the orders but never watches. (*Pause*)

HOESS (*Encouraging, now digging*) Surely there must be more? What you have told me is all run-of-the-mill. What about his watching the men taking showers?

KRAMER (*Missing the point*) Yes, he does that. (*Hoess realises now he is wasting his time with Kramer. Kramer obviously doesn't get the point that Hoess has suspicions that Steiner is a homosexual.*)

HOESS (*Terminating the interview*) Thank you for coming. Good day. (*Kramer gets up, puts on his cap, salutes, marches out like a wooden rooster and shuts the door very cautiously. Hoess leaves his swivel chair, places his hands behind his back, paces up and down very slowly, deep in thought. The shunting and chugging of trains is heard in the distance with an occasional whistle blast. All the time Hoess chain smokes, seemingly on edge. He goes over to the phone, dials in a few numbers, barks into the receiver: 'Bring me my trestle and my board'. A minute passes whilst Hoess stares fascinated at the blow-up of Hitler. The door opens and two guards enter. One carries a blackboard on which are drawn a number of graphic lines like a business sales chart. The other carries in a trestle. Hoess, indicating:* Set it up over there behind my desk. *The two guards set up the blackboard and trestle and leave. A short pause whilst Hoess slightly adjusts the board to his liking. The duty corporal enters.*)

DUTY CORPORAL You sent for Second Lieutenant Steiner, Herr Kommandant?

HOESS (*Throwing off his apparent fug*) Yes. Show him in. (*We hear the duty corporal speak. 'Please go in.' Steiner's voice, 'Thank you, Corporal.' Steiner enters, approaches Hoess, salutes very smartly.*)

STEINER (*Respectfully*) You wish to see me, Herr Hoess? (*Hoess nods, indicates for Steiner to sit.*)

HOESS   (*Friendly*) Make yourself comfortable. (*Steiner sits down, removes his cap, places it on his lap.*)

STEINER   (*Pleasantly*) I believe that Emmi celebrates her birthday tomorrow. (*Hoess smiles*) May I convey my best wishes?

HOESS   (*Pleased*) Thank you, Steiner. (*Very slight pause. Hoess is sizing Steiner up carefully*) Should you wish to join Frau Hoess and my family tomorrow night for Emmi's party, you will be most welcome. Captain Kleinsmidt will be there and some other officers. I'm sure Captain Kleinsmidt can arrange for you to take the time off. You report to him, not so?

STEINER   (*Politely*) He is my superior officer, yes. Unfortunately for myself, I shall have to decline your invitation as my reports are very much behind and I shall have to catch up. Thank you, however, Herr Hoess for your kind invitation and my apologies to Emmi and Frau Hoess. (*Hoess is not happy with Steiner's refusal of his invitation. His jaw muscles tense. But he manages to control his anger at the snub and draws deeply on his cigarette. He suspects now that Steiner is indeed a loner and unsociable. But he has had no confirmation of his homosexuality, so he dismisses it from his suspicions and decides to win Steiner over.*)

HOESS   (*Removing a letter from a drawer*) You wrote me this confidential letter, marking it clearly for my eyes only. You realise, of course, that the correct course of action is to put your request through Captain Kleinsmidt as your line officer. I should have discussed this matter with Kleinsmidt, but decided against it and respect your confidentiality. However, I must inform you that should your request be approved, one way or the other, your superior officer, Kleinsmidt, will have to know about it. Understood?

STEINER (*Nods*) Understood.

HOESS Good. (*Very slight pause as he runs his eyes quickly over the letter*). Now, Steiner, your request. Let's evaluate it. (*Very slight pause*) You were unable to attend your mother's funeral in Berlin after she was killed in an enemy bombing raid as you were on the Russian front serving with the Einsatzgruppen. Since your transfer here, you have not seen your father for several years. (*Pause*) I offer you my sympathy for your mother's death, Steiner. A terrible loss for anyone. Death of a family member is always very sad. (*Pause. He scans letter again*). Auschwitz, as you know, Steiner, is not a place from which anyone can take a leave of absence. Transfer from here only goes to one place . . . the Russian front. As for leave to see family or friends, it is strictly verbotten. I'm sure you can understand the reasons. Serving here demands total and complete dedication to the Reich. (*Pause*) However, Steiner, in your case I am prepared to forward your request directly to Reichsführer Himmler himself. I understand he is acquainted with your family. Your father and the Reichsführer were once school friends. (*Steiner nods slightly. He is unhappy that family connections form part of the approval of his request, but he is not a fool and knows the system, so he lets Hoess continue. Hoess forces geniality.)* Not so?

STEINER   That is so, Herr Hoess. My father and Reichsführer Himmler go back a long way. Twenty or more years. *(Hoess smiles as warmly as he can)* They went to the same school in Berlin. *(Steiner smiles)*

HOESS   *(Sugary)* In fact, I will phone the Reichsführer in addition to sending him your letter.

STEINER   Thank you.

HOESS   *(Smilingly)* A pleasure, Steiner. Ah, Berlin. I must confess I envy you a trip there. But with our performance here, I'm expecting a trip very soon. Yes, very soon. *(Pause)*

STEINER   Appreciated, Herr Hoess. *(He begins to get up)* May I go now?

HOESS   *(Waving him down)* A few more minutes before you go, Steiner. *(Steiner remains seated. Hoess puts the letter back in a drawer. He takes out a fresh pack of cigarettes, relaxes, settles down for a discussion . . . father-to-son type.)* So you wish to have a talk, Steiner? *(Steiner frowns, shifts uncomfortably . . . What's coming?)*

STEINER   *(Unsure of the invitation to talk)* Herr Hoess? *(Hoess, chain smoking, reaches behind him, pulls out one of the filing cabinet drawers, swivels back, removes a bottle of Schnapps and two glasses, places them on the desk, pours.)* I don't quite follow.

HOESS   *(Fatherly)* Here, Steiner. *(Hands him schnapps)*

Relax. (*Hoess knocks back the schnapps. Steiner sips slowly*).

STEINER Thank you. Most unexpected, but thank you.

HOESS (*Aware of Steiner's connections higher up, speaks slowly*) Look, Steiner. I am not a fool. For a man of your background it cannot be an easy task being here. (*Steiner listens attentively*) When I came to Auschwitz, I saw the big picture, Steiner. I saw what the final solution was all about. We have a great task to sweep Europe clean. We cannot focus on moral issues, Steiner. Your background creates those kinds of problems. I understand. (*Pause*) You know when your file arrived on my desk, I was very pleased. An officer for me from the Russian front, from the Einsatzgruppen, what a catch to have! But I thought to myself, why is this man still an Untersturmführer, a Second Lieutenant? Then I saw the notation – 'suffering stress'. And I wondered how this man, you, Steiner, would fit in here. (*Pause*) To be frank, Steiner, there are concerns. (*Steiner is about to speak, but Hoess waves a upturned hand*) Let me finish, Steiner. These concerns are that you find it hard going. Now, Steiner, that's no crime. We all find it hard. Every day I have to worry about the logistics, the late trains, the paperwork, the lack of boxcars, the demands from Berlin, the sheer number of arrivals to be treated appropriately. It makes my home life difficult when I have to return home to Frau Hoess and listen to her complaints about the servants and to find time to play with my dear sweet children. Sometimes

Frau Hoess chides me. 'What are we going to do when the war is over? People are going to ask questions about your work at Auschwitz. What are you going to tell them?' 'Tell them, I ask? What do you mean, what am I going to tell them?' I reply to Frau Hoess, 'My darling, I'm going to tell them the truth.' Of course, Steiner, we do not run a sanatorium at Auschwitz. We run a humane institution according to the rules of State policy. What is so terrible about the gas chamber? It only takes from three to fifteen minutes to put the victims to sleep. Look how efficient it all is, Steiner. Half an hour after the screaming stops, the bodies are removed. The special commandos remove the rings and gold teeth and cut off the hair. Minutes later the other special commandos put the bodies into the ovens. A hard task, Steiner. Those fires have to be stoked; all the fat has to be drained off; all those corpses have to be turned over so that the draught can fan the flames. Think of all the tasks involved. If we were not efficient, Steiner, how could we cope? Some day, Steiner, the world will marvel at how productive we were. If only we had better rail timetables. So you see, Steiner, I understand why you find those onerous tasks hard. I would too. I hate going over to the crematoriums. I hate watching executions and punishments. I even hate having to front up at the ramp every day. I hate having to talk to Mengele, he is always so smug, so superior. What the doctor doesn't realise is that we have to do all the mechanics of running this place. We have a lot in common, Steiner . . . We see the big picture. No wonder you were stressed in the Einsatzgruppen. Such an unsophisticated way to do things. Shooting vermin in the back of the head and having the brains and blood spilled all over one's uniform. (*Pause*). Go to Berlin, Steiner. See your father. Relax. Listen to your favourite music. See your friends. Come back refreshed. Then begin anew. I have big plans for you, Steiner. Big plans. Look at this. (*Hoess gets up. Stands in front of the blackboard and easel. Takes a pencil. Indicates*). See this line, Steiner? That's our target. See this line above it? That's our level of performance. Last week we processed ten thousand in one day. One day, Steiner! Treblinka, Dachau, Buchenwald, Belsec, and all those other camps cannot match our record. Why, only yesterday, the call came through from Berlin from Eichmann congratulating me. I took out a bottle of schnapps and polished it off. Wonderful work, said Eichmann, ten thousand in a single day! 'Fantastic, Hoess', he said, 'keep it up. The Führer will be very happy.' What do you think of that, hey Steiner? Gut, yah? Gut! (*Smiles, waits anxiously for Steiner's response*)

STEINER (*Tiredly, a bit cynically*) Very commendable, Herr Hoess.

HOESS (*Getting carried away*) When you get back from Berlin, I'm going to put you in charge of a special unit, Steiner. A man with your education, your background, is wasted in crematorium duties, executions, punishments. What you need is stimulus, Steiner! (*He moves from the blackboard, sits down again, pours a large schnapps for himself, gulps it down.*) Ah, gut. (*Very slight pause*) Now, as I was saying, Steiner, a special unit. What I have in mind is for you to take command of the co-ordination of the rail traffic from the East. I . . . (*An urgent knock on the door interrupts Hoess. He barks.*) Ja?! (*The duty corporal enters, his eyes wide, alert, excited*) Berlin on the line, Herr Kommandant! I believe it's the Führer himself! (*Hoess snatches up the phone. Listens. Waves anxiously to Steiner to get up and leave. Clapping his hand over the mouthpiece, he whispers loudly to Steiner as he gets up to leave*) Thank you, Steiner, for coming. We will talk again. (*Steiner puts on his cap, salutes, turns and leaves.*) Yes? Yes . . . Hoess here! (*It is a bad line. The operator is telling him the line is too bad, the Führer is impatient and cannot wait. He will write a letter instead. Hoess becomes a picture of disappointment. He empties the schnapps bottle, gulps it down straight from the bottle. Then he realises he is still holding the phone in his hand and slowly replaces it. His voice is full of disappointment as he gets up and turns to stare at his blackboard graphs.*) The Führer himself, Adolf Hitler . . . (*His voice trails off as the light slowly fades into darkness. Far off, the chugging and shunting of trains is heard. A fairly prolonged whistle, almost haunting sounds, heralding yet another trainload of new arrivals at the ramp.*)

The light rises in the block. The stage is empty. It is very cold. The time, close

to eight-thirty, evening. The door crashes open. The inmates shuffle in exhausted.
Louie is the last to enter, followed by Hans. Louie limps. His ankles are swollen,
his feet sore and blistered. He goes over to one of the box chairs, sits down, removes
his broken boots, massages his sore feet. The other inmates retreat to their bunks
to lie down. Hans, seeing Louie in distress, comes over to him. The light shifts
and focuses in a circle round Louie and Hans. The bunks fall into darkness. Some
inmates are heard coughing from damaged lungs. In the distance again the shunting
noises of trains. Music from the Auschwitz Band is heard . . . 'Wien, Wien,
Nur du Allein'. Hans sits down at Louie's feet, very gently takes hold of them
and rubs them.

HANS I will get some shoes for you from the warehouse
tomorrow.

LOUIE (*Annoyed*) You always make promises. Where's
my chicken?

HANS (*Defensively*) What's more important . . .chicken
or shoes? (*Louie shoves Hans' hands off his feet, pulls*
them up as he bends his knees and clasps his arms
around his knees. He is clearly angry at Hans.)

HANS (*Hurt*) What have I done, my little angel? Did I
hurt you? (*Trying hard to please*) Let me get some
water and wash them for you.

LOUIE (*Firmly*) No. Leave me alone. Go away.

HANS (*Pleading, almost desperate*) Tomorrow I promise I
will bring you chicken. (*He removes a greasy piece*
of cloth from his clothing, unwraps it) Look. (*He offers*
the contents for Louie to look at)

LOUIE (*Interested but puzzled*) What is it?

HANS (*Proudly*) Gold teeth. Five of them.

LOUIE (*Unimpressed*) So . . .? (*Hans wraps up the cloth,*
returns it to his pocket)

HANS (*Anxious to please*) With these I can get chicken for you. Do you want white meat or brown? (*Louie bursts out laughing. He laughs for quite a while, then his laughter subsides and he shakes his head to indicate how silly Hans' question was*)

LOUIE (*Tauntingly*) White meat or brown meat? (*Imitating Hans and doing a waiter's pantomime*) Sir . . .do you wish to have the white meat or the brown meat . . . or perhaps, sir, you prefer both? (*He laughs again, but this time it is a forced laugh. Hans stands dejectedly now, he looks forlorn and defeated. Louie carries on with his pantomime*) What about some white wine with your chicken, sir? In France we have excellent wines . . . red and white. With chicken, of course, sir, you would prefer white. I'll see to it that . . . (*Hans lunges forward and slaps Louie. Louie retreats backwards in shock, holds his hand to his cheek. Hans, realising what he has done, rushes forward and puts his arms around Louie.*)

(*Author's note: Louie's accent is strongly French, therefore, wine sounds like whine etc*)

HANS (*Pathetically*) Oh, my little angel. My little darling. My little bird with the broken wings. I'm sorry! I'm sorry! I'm sorry! Forgive me, my little darling! (*He begins to sob*) Forgive me! Forgive me! (*Louie breaks free, pushes Hans from him. Hans, sobbing, falls on his knees moaning with unhappiness, clutches Louie's feet*)

LOUIE (*Not falling for Hans's sobbing. A case of 'cry wolf' too often*) Get up!

HANS   (*Pleading, kisses Louie's feet*) I get you shoes, chicken, another jacket, anything. (*Agonising*) I love you, Louie. I love you!

LOUIE   (*Softening*) All right. Get up. Go to bed. You don't have to fetch rations tonight. They fed us bread and soup in the factory. The new supervisor told us we were to get more food so that we can keep working the machines. And you, you never go to bed hungry. Look how fat you are. Like an old pig. You're fat like an old pig because you steal food all day and shove it into your mouth like it was never going to get full. (*Hans gets up. He is smiling now. He feels Louie has forgiven him.*)

HANS   (*Seizing the opportunity, warming up to Louie again*) Just like an old pig! (*Laughs*). Just like an old pig! (*Then, appealing to Louie's now softened demeanour*) But you love this old pig! Not so? Not so?

LOUIE   (*Impatiently*) Yes, yes. Go to bed now. I want to sit here by myself and massage my feet. (*The door opens. Both turn towards the sound. A figure is seen approaching. It comes into the circle of light. It is an SS private. He throws a parcel on to the floor. It is wrapped in brown paper and tied with string. Louie and Hans stand and stare transfixed. What is this they are both thinking?*)

SS PRIVATE   (*Contemptuously*) Something for the French boy from Untersturmführer Steiner.

HANS   (*Curious*) What is it? (*Louie bends down and lifts the parcel. He stares at it as though he has never seen a parcel before. The SS private has ignored Hans' question, he too is more interested in watching the parcel*

and Louie's reaction to it. Hans repeats his question.)
What is in the parcel? (*Again ignored, he turns to
Louie*) Open it.

LOUIE (*Quite defiantly*) No. It's for me. I'll open it alone.
(*The SS private smiles at Louie and turns to go. He
has other things to do.*)

HANS (*Shouts to the SS private as he leaves, now very
anxiously, very insistently, fearing to be left out by
Louie*) What's in the parcel?! (*The SS private stops
at the door and calls back to Hans in a joking voice:*
'Maybe poison for you Jews'. *He shuts the door
behind him. As he opens the door to exit, the sound
of barking dogs is heard quite loudly. Coarse rough
commands of sentries. Louie has not opened his parcel.
He is waiting for Hans to leave, to leave him alone.
He stands quietly with the parcel tucked tightly against
his chest. Hans, though, is determined to hang around.*)

HANS (*Looking as closely as he can at the parcel*) Looks like
food inside. (*Louie is not going to budge*)

LOUIE (*Encouragingly*) Why don't you go to bed?

HANS (*Loudly, acting up, trying to ingratiate himself again*)
Did you hear what that SS swine said? (*Voices
from the bunks:* 'Shut up! Keep quiet! We're trying
to rest'.) He said, it's poison for us Jews. Sick
bastard swine! Shithead!

LOUIE Go to bed.

HANS Will you come too?

LOUIE No.

HANS (*Angry now*) It's that parcel isn't it? It's because
you don't want to share the food inside.

LOUIE (*Impatiently*) It isn't food. (*Jokes*) It's full of Zyklon B.

HANS (*Sarcastically*) Very funny. (*Louie sits down on one of the box chairs, still clutching the parcel to his chest*)

LOUIE (*Being nice*) Go to your bed now. I will show you in the morning. (*Hans is now boiling with suspicion. It's no more a question of curiosity. Something's up. In the past there were never secrets between them. Why now?*)

HANS (*Taking on a tougher line*) There's no time in the morning. Show me now.

LOUIE (*Stubbornly*) No. (*Hans moves closer to Louie. He takes on the look of someone preparing himself for quick action.*)

HANS (*Sneeringly*) Steiner and you were up to something. That parcel's his reward to you. I bet he's been making passes at you. I saw how he looks at you. He wants you for a bit of fun. Just a bit of fun. Not love, just something to play with. Yes, you're to be his little Kroliky, his little guinea pig.

LOUIE (*Angry now*) You're jealous. (*Very slight pause*) Go away, go to your bed. Leave me alone. (*Suddenly, Hans lunges forward, snatches the parcel from Louie. They grapple, but Hans is too powerful, he waltzes his huge frame in defensive movements keeping Louie helplessly trying to reach the parcel. Hans rips it open, tearing it apart with brute strength. A pair of shoes falls on the floor. Louie manages to crawl through Hans' legs, snatches up shoes. Hans bursts out laughing, indicating the shoes. *)

HANS Just a pair of shoes! (*He continues to laugh*

uproariously, staggering like a drunken sailor to his bunk. As he goes into the darkness enveloping the bunks a circle of light floods around Louie standing holding the shoes to his bosom very protectively. For a few minutes Louie stands quietly as though he were holding the most precious shoes in the whole world. Well, in his world, he is. Intermittently we hear Hans conversing with himself, 'Only a stupid pair of shoes. A stupid pair of shoes . . .' *Louie very slowly goes over to one of the box chairs and sits down. He kisses each shoe very tenderly in turn, and rubs each one very gently against his face, relishing the feeling of having such a wonderful thing; not old, broken, cast off, three-sizes-too-large boots, but a pair of real leather shoes. Slowly, very gently, he puts on the shoes. He smiles, marvels. They fit! He gets up, walks to and fro very slowly, admiring the shoes. Very slowly the light begins to fade as Louie returns to his chair and very gradually, very gently, proceeds to remove his precious shoes. It is almost dark now. We suddenly hear, quite loud this time, the shunting of trains, box cars being coupled, dogs barking, coarse voices barking commands, the haunting voices of children crying. Then suddenly, silence. As total darkness descends now, the strains of* 'Wien, Wien, Nur du allein'.)

LOUIE   (*In the darkness, with great feeling, sings a haunting little song in French.*)

I want to walk away
With my shoes,
To places far away,
To mama, and papa.
Take me there,

To places far away,
To rivers, and fields of flowers,
To Paris.
To home, and love,
For ever –
Take me there,
Please take me there...

Light rises in the block. The bunks are empty. All the inmates have left for their work assignments some hours beforehand. Kramer enters. He looks agitated, worried. He paces backwards and forwards. He shuts the door. He has shaky hands. Kramer (to himself, stressed: 'How could I do such a stupid thing?') We see the door open slightly. Steiner peers in, then seeing Kramer, he enters.

STEINER   One of your men said you wish to speak with me privately and that you would meet me here. (*Very slight pause*) What is it about? (*Kramer runs his tongue over his lips. He is tensed up.*)

KRAMER   I did something very stupid. If Herr Hoess finds out, it will be straight to the Russian front for me. (*Almost desperately*) Can you help me please, Herr Steiner? (*Steiner frowns. He is surprised at the intensity of Kramer's apparent distress for such a tough operator, who would never hesitate to carry out the most brutal of tasks.*)

STEINER   Would you like a cigarette? (*Takes out pack*)

KRAMER   (*Worried*) In here?

STEINER   We are alone. (*Kramer bites his lips*)

KRAMER   (*Relents*) All right. Thank you. (*Steiner shakes out a cigarette, takes one for himself. Lights his own first, then Kramer's. They smoke.*)

STEINER   Now, what is the problem with Herr Hoess?

KRAMER (*Very anxiously, tensed as he now has to open up*)
It's not a problem directly connected with Kommandant Hoess. (*He stalls*) It's . . . it's his daughter.

STEINER (*Puzzled*) His daughter? How?

KRAMER (*Nervously*) You won't like it. (*Stalls again*)

STEINER (*Patiently*) Go on. Whether I like it or not, you must get it off your chest. I can see you are troubled by whatever happened. .

KRAMER *(Anxiously)* Do I have your word as a German officer that it will go no further? (*Pause. Steiner does not yet respond*) We do not like one another, Herr Steiner. I know that. You are an educated man, an officer. I am just a stupid soldier trying to do his best. But of all the officers here, you are the only one I would trust. I can see you are a soldier and a gentleman. So, I have your word? (*Steiner weighs up the situation very thoughtfully for awhile, then decides he will agree to give Kramer his word of silence.*)

STEINER (*Sincerely*) You have my word. (*Kramer pulls deeply on his cigarette. His hands are clammy, he rubs them off against his trousers. He struggles to stand still*)

KRAMER (*Confessionally, slowly*) Yesterday – it was late afternoon – Captain Kleinsmidt called me to his office and told me to take two men over to Kommandant Hoess's House. We were to collect some cases of champagne left over from his daughter's birthday party. We went to the house. The Kommandant was not there, but Frau Hoess was there. I reported to her and told her we had come to fetch the cases of champagne. She took us to the cellar. There were many bottles lying all over the place. Bottles out of cases and so forth. So I told my two men to put the bottles in cases and tidy up. I left them and went outside for a smoke. There was a passage running alongside the house, a pathway, you know, between the house and a wall. I decided to walk down it. I was bored with such a menial detail, collecting bottles, leftover bottles of champagne. As I walked down the passage I passed a window. The curtains were open. I looked in. And there, standing in front of the mirror looking at herself, was one of Herr Hoess's daughters. I stood to one side so that she couldn't see me and I peeped at her. You know, like a peeping tom. I couldn't pull myself away. She looked so beautiful, so fresh, so clean. I don't know what came over me, Herr Steiner. My feet became lead. I couldn't move away. It was terrible. Terrible! (*Almost on the verge of tears*). What a mess! What a mess! (*His voice trails off . . .*)

STEINER (*Sympathetically*) Get a hold of yourself. It doesn't sound so bad. You are a peeping tom, that's all. Did anyone see you there?

KRAMER (*Stubbing out his cigarette*) You have not heard the rest, Herr Steiner . . .

STEINER Go on. (*Kramer takes a deep breath, exhales tensely, slowly, he shakes his head in a self deprecating manner.*)

KRAMER (*Hesitantly*) You see . . . she was . . . she was . . . naked.

STEINER (*Surprised*) Naked?

KRAMER (*Quickly*) Yes, yes, naked. (*Steiner stubs his cigarette.*)

STEINER (*Considering thoughtfully now*) Hmmm . . .

KRAMER (*Desperately*) Can you help me? Can you help me? I cannot go to the Russian front. If I go, I will never come back alive. I know it. I don't want to die. I have a girl in Munich. She and I want to marry when the war is over. We want to buy a small farm together. We want to keep cows and chickens and rabbits and maybe even a horse. We'll make our own cheese from milk and cream so thick you will have to cut it with a knife. And . . . and we'll have children. Nice, clean, wholesome German children, children just like the Führer will want us to have . . . I . . .

STEINER (*Interrupting*) Is that the full story Kramer, or is there more? Did you just stand there watching a naked girl like a peeping tom and nobody saw you? Is it a question of clearing your conscience or is there more? (*Firmly*) Come on man, is that all?

KRAMER (*Hangdog*) No. There's more.

STEINER What?

KRAMER Can I have another cigarette? (*Steiner shakes out another cigarette and returns the packet to his pocket. He hands Kramer the box of matches. Kramer lights up, draws deeply, exhales a cloud of smoke. The cigarette has now become a crutch. He smokes desperately.*)

STEINER (*After a pause*) Take your time, Kramer, but tell me everything. If you want my help, I must know everything. (*Kramer swallows hard. He has a*

*deep inner conflict, he feels trapped, desperate, but
realises there is no way out now. Like it or not, the
moment of truth has arrived)*

KRAMER (*Guiltily*) I masturbated. (*A fairly long pause. Steiner
is trying to weigh up this confession, which has now
put a new angle on things.*)

STEINER (*Quietly*) She saw you?

KRAMER (*Agonising*) Yes. She came to the window.

STEINER What did she do?

KRAMER (*Painfully*) She – she watched me.

STEINER (*Trying to understand and be sympathetic*) You did
not move away? Cover yourself? (*Kramer is sweat-
ing profusely, wringing his hands, tormented by the
recollection of his misdemeanour*)

KRAMER (*Desperately*) Oh God, it was terrible! I couldn't
help myself! I couldn't stop!

STEINER All the time she watched?

KRAMER (*Unable to keep still, agonising*) Yes! Yes!
Yes! (*Pause, starting to crack up*) She was smiling.
Smiling at me as though she was saying – carry
on – continue – I am enjoying it too. (*Putting
his hands to his head, tugging his hair*). If she tells
Herr Hoess, I'm finished, Steiner. (*He controls
himself*). I'm sorry, Herr Steiner, I'm finished . . .
finished! (*Pause. Kramer pats his hair back into place*)

STEINER (*Patiently, gently prompting*) How did it end? What
happened when you had finished relieving yourself? Did she draw the curtains, and then you left?
What? (*Kramer wipes the perspiration off his face and*

neck. *Wipes his clammy hands on his trousers. Grinds his cigarette under his heel.*)

KRAMER *(Calmer now)* She held her breasts in her hands, pushing them against the glass. Then she laughed at me and drew the curtains quickly. I think someone was coming to her room. *(Pause. Then hurt)* She was making fun of me. *(Kramer seems to relax now that the confession with Steiner has come to an end. In a quiet, but still desperate voice)* What am I to do? Hoess *(corrects himself)* Kommandant Herr Hoess will maybe have me shot. *(Pause)*

STEINER No one saw you? No one? Are you sure of it?

KRAMER *(Positively)* Yes, I am sure of it. No one. It was just the two of us. *(Pause)*

STEINER *(With empathy)* It can happen to anyone. It was a moment of weakness. Forget about it. Get on with your work. Don't go near the Kommandant's house ever again. Understood?

KRAMER *(Desperate, clutching for reassurance)* But what if she tells her father? *(Pause)*

STEINER *(Considering, then with confidence)* I doubt that she will. She never yelled at you. She did not call out for help. She enjoyed it. If she didn't, all hell would have broken out and you most likely would have been facing a court martial or a firing squad by now.

KRAMER *(Anxiously, wanting to believe)* You really think so? You really think that she enjoyed it, just played games with me?

STEINER Yes. Forget it.

KRAMER She will not go to her father?

STEINER No, I doubt she will. Now go. Put it behind you. (*Kramer looks decidedly relieved. A faint smile of relief crosses his face. He looks directly at Steiner now. Their eyes meet.*)

KRAMER (*Genuinely with feeling*) I am grateful to you, Herr Steiner, for hearing me out. (*Very slight pause*) You have listened to me. No one else in this camp would have done so. And besides, Herr Steiner, I trust you. I know that what I have told you will remain with you. (*A very slight pause*) If there is anything I can do for you in return, Herr Steiner, you have only to ask. (*Very slight pause*) Is there anything I can do in return?

STEINER (*Decently*) No, Kramer. A man sometimes needs to talk. You and I have done so. It is enough. Should I ever need your help, I shall remember your offer. Go now, before someone comes and perceives something that they would like to perceive.

KRAMER (*Gratefully*) You are right, Herr Steiner. The camp is full of spies. Not one of us can trust another. (*Pause*) But you – you are different from the others.

STEINER (*Uncomfortable*) Thank you for your comments, Kramer. (*Forcefully*) Now go. That is an order!

KRAMER (*Ever grateful*) Thank you! (*He exits quickly. The door shuts. Steiner looks relieved. He takes out a cigarette and lights it. For a moment or two he stands smoking, contemplating the events just brought out by Kramer. In the distance the trains are chugging and shunting. He listens for a moment, thoughtfully, then*

63

*he slowly walks to the door, opens it halfway, looks
back into the block. An unhappy look crosses his face.
God, he thinks to himself, is this what my life has
come to? He leaves heavily. The door shuts behind
him. Slowly the light fades into darkness.)*

*The light slowly rises. Hoess and Kleinsmidt are giving an informal get-together
of junior SS Officers in Hoess's office. Steiner is noticeably absent. There are
glasses, bottles of champagne and a tray of sandwiches on the desk. The huge
blow-up of Adolf Hitler again separates the office from the bunks, which are in
darkness. Light focuses over the gathering. Rather loud small talk amongst everyone.
Kleinsmidt and Hoess are standing a few feet apart behind the desk, the junior
officers on the other side. Each person is holding a glass of champagne. Hoess taps
a ruler on the desk to draw attention. Everyone present falls silent.*

HOESS *(The toastmaster. He raises his glass to the blow-up
of Hitler)*: To the Führer. *(All present raise their
glasses to the blow-up portrait.)* Heil Hitler!

KLEINSMIDT AND   Heil Hitler! *(They drink the toast)*
OFFICERS IN CHORUS

HOESS *(Waits a moment for their enthusiasm to settle)*
Gentlemen, thank you for coming. *(Indicating
bottles of champagne and food)* As you can see, this
is not a formal meeting. It is good sometimes just
to get together and talk. Tonight, however, I
must intrude a little into our social life. I am
going to hand you over now to Captain Kleinsmidt to give you more details.

(During this meeting Hoess refrains from smoking.)

KLEINSMIDT *(Adjusting his tunic, clearing his throat)* Thank you,
Herr Kommandant. *(Speaking clearly and deliber-
ately)* I do not need to remind you what a great

responsibility we here, at Auschwitz, have towards our Fatherland, our beloved Führer and
the Third Reich. Tomorrow, an inspector from
Reichsführer Himmler will be paying us a visit
from Berlin. The Reichsführer, Herr Himmler,
is attending to other important affairs and cannot
unfortunately, pay us a visit this time. (*Murmurs
of disappointment*) Yes, gentlemen, the Kommandant and myself share your disappointment. But
that is how matters stand. (*Pause*) Now. There
are some deficiencies in our operation which we
do not want reported back to Berlin. (*Pause*) Let
me give you some examples. A few days ago I
was present on the ramp during the selection
process. I was forced to reprimand a doctor for
saying to a new group of arrivals: 'you have come
to a concentration camp, not a sanatorium, so do
not ask for my help if you are sick. There is only
one way out of here: (*he indicates*) up the chimney.' (*Laughter from the officers. Hoess taps his ruler
for order*). Let me continue. 'Yes', he added, 'only
one way, unless you prefer hanging yourself on
the electric wires. No Jews have the right to live
more than two weeks; nuns and priests one
month. The rest of you who are fit enough to
work, three months, that is if you're lucky'.
(*Laughter again. Hoess taps his ruler for order*) Please,
gentlemen, as much as we enjoy our work, and
a bit of laughter is good for the stomach, I must
remind you of Reichsführer Himmler's policy.
To repeat. We must keep our victims pliable.
There should be no anxiety-producing revelations

until such time as they are inside the shower rooms and looking up at the tiny blue pellets falling on them like raindrops – (*Smiles, jokes now*) flowers from heaven – sorry, Zyklon B from heaven. (*Laughter, this time with Hoess and Kleinsmidt joining in. A few moments of laughter continue, then Kleinsmidt raises his hand and the laughter subsides. Kleinsmidt takes a sip of champagne. The officers shift in their seats, the meeting comes to order again*) You men working at the showers have a special responsibility. The signs leading to the showers reading 'To the showers', are, as you all know, the brilliant idea of our Kommandant. (*Hoess beams. The officers clap. Kleinsmidt waits for the applause to die down, adjusts his tie, continues*) Remember our Reichsführer's word, gentlemen – pliability – pliability. I will give a demonstration. (*He now goes into a pantomime, stepping away from the desk, acting in front of an audience*) 'Ah, good morning, welcome to the showers. (*Smiles from Hoess and the officers*) Yes, to answer your question. You will now be bathed and disinfected so that we don't get any epidemics in the camp. After your shower you will be taken to your barracks where you will get some warm soup and bread and afterwards you will be put to work utilizing your skills. Yes, yes, that's right. Get undressed here and put your clothes down in front of you. Yes, that's right, put your shoes next to your clothes so that you can find them again after the shower. Is the water warm? Of course! Warm, invigorating water to refresh you after your long journey. What is your trade? Oh, yes, carpenter. Very good. We need them urgently. Please report to me right afterwards. Right, I see you are now undressed. Good. This way. The showers are right here. Just follow me through this tunnel'. (*Kleinsmidt bows. Loud clapping at this fine theatrical performance*)

HOESS (*Smiling ear to ear*) Wunderbar! Wunderbar! (*The applause slowly subsides. Kleinsmidt raises his hand in acknowledgement of the applause*)

KLEINSMIDT Thank you. Thank you. (*Returns behind desk. Pause*)

HOESS (*To Kleinsmidt, smiling*) A man of many talents. (*Then to officers who are now all alert, eyes shining, eager to carry out their fiendish tasks*) Any questions? (*A hand is raised. A young twenty-year-old, SS junior officer stands up*) Yes, Möller, what do you wish to ask?

MÖLLER (*Addressing Kleinsmidt*) With respect, Herr Kleinsmidt, how are we going to cope with the huge numbers of Jews arriving day and night? Our gas chambers and our crematoriums are working twenty-four hours a day. Our mass graves are filling up. Cannot the other camps take more?

HOESS (*Agitated, looks at Kleinsmidt. Their eyes meet and he glares back at Möller, clearly unhappy with Möller's question*) I will answer Second Lieutenant Möller's question, Captain Kleinsmidt. (*Hoess wets his lips*) When one runs a business, one doesn't turn away customers. We have targets to meet. (*Gets carried away again*) Our camp has the finest production records of all the other camps put together. We do not worry about such small problems. There is plenty of space in Auschwitz for mass graves. We are going to install more ovens. We should be concentrating our efforts on production – production, not a lot of negative rubbish. What I want, Möller, is to intensify our selection process, cut back more on rations, give more labour to the factories. Nothing, Möller, succeeds like good management. As a German, Möller, you should know that everything depends on efficiency. Is that clear? (*Möller wishes there was a hole to swallow him up. A pained look crosses his baby face*).

MÖLLER   Thank you, mein Kommandant. (*He sits*)

KLEINSMIDT   Well, gentlemen. That will be all. Thank you for coming. Back to your duties. (*The officers get up, each in turn nod a salute, click their heels together and exit. Some laughter, some talk amongst themselves as they leave. Kleinsmidt moves to sit opposite Hoess who now sits at his desk.*)

HOESS   (*Lights up now and chain smokes*) Möller needs a kick up the arse. (*Kleinsmidt pours more champagne, sips slowly, relishing every sip*)

KLEINSMIDT   He's only a baby. Came straight to Auschwitz and has never been to the front lines.

HOESS   (*Surprised*) Ag so? So why is he here?

KLEINSMIDT   Relative of the Heyndrich family and connected to Göring.

HOESS   (*Sharply*) My God! You should have warned me! Now the little weasel may talk. Göring! My promotion will be history! If I'd known, I would have kissed his arse, not kicked it!

KLEINSMIDT (*Reassuringly*) Leave it with me. I'll soften it over. I'll move him from the shower duty and put him with Steiner.

HOESS Thank you. (*Pause*) Speaking of Steiner, I must let you know he has requested leave, a few days, to go to Berlin. A family matter. You know, his father is very well connected – right to the top. Any objections to that?

KLEINSMIDT (*A bit taken aback*) Well . . . it's contrary to policy. The danger of loose talk . . .

HOESS Steiner's all right. In any case, who would believe him if he does talk?

KLEINSMIDT (*Sceptical*) There are enemies of the Reich in Berlin who might be prepared to listen. I don't like the idea of any officer going out of here.

HOESS (*Impatient*) God, Kleinsmidt! Can't you understand my position? Steiner is not an ordinary officer. His father knows the Führer personally. His mother was a famous pianist. She used to play the piano at the Führer's birthday. (*Agitated*) Between you and Möller, it seems that in spite of my fantastic work here, I'm not going to get my promotion to Berlin!

KLEINSMIDT (*Apologetically*) I'm sorry, Herr Hoess. I did not mean to upset you. It's just that one of the mainstays of our operation is complete secrecy. Our work is of such vital importance.

HOESS (*Irritably*) Yes, yes, Kleinsmidt, I know. I do not

need to be lectured on what I already know. What I am concerned with is that, whether you like it or not, or whether I like it or not, Steiner must go to Berlin. Understood?

KLEINSMIDT (*A bit wearily*) Very well, Herr Hoess, Herr Kommandant. If those are your orders (*Getting up*) When does he wish to leave?

HOESS Let him go the day after tomorrow.

KLEINSMIDT Will that be all, Herr Kommandant?

HOESS (*Pouting, sulky*) Yes. (*Kleinsmidt puts on his cap, salutes with an extra sharp click of his heels, turns and exits. The door shuts. Hoess lights another cigarette, downs a half glass of champagne in one gulp. He sits moodily. His teeth ache. He rubs them vigorously. He airs his complaints to himself*) Surrounded by fools. Fools who cannot understand planning, organization, productivity. What do they know . . .? Nothing but a bunch of uniformed robots. What would Himmler, Eichmann, do without me . . .? (*The light very slowly fades on Hoess, chain smoking, blowing out circles of smoke.*)

It is early morning. The inmates have left for work, all except for Louie. He is lying in his bunk asleep. The door opens and Hans comes in quickly and goes over to Louie. He shakes Louie awake.

HANS (*Agitated*) Why weren't you at roll call?

LOUIE (*Plaintively*) My feet are too sore. (*Louie is barefoot*)

HANS (*Anxiously*) Well, wear your shoes. Come. Hurry. Come before the guards come looking for you.

LOUIE (*Stubbornly*) No. My shoes are not for work. They are special. If I work – I wear my boots.

HANS   (*Pleading*) For God's sake get up! (*Heavy footsteps are heard coming closer. Voices. Hans goes quickly to the door, carefully, cautiously looks out, rushes back to Louie. Breathlessly he urges, pleads with Louie*) The guards are coming to inspect the blocks! Hurry, we can still get out! (*Tugs Louie's sleeve*)

LOUIE   (*Indifferent*) You go. (*Shoves Hans' hand off his sleeve*)

HANS   (*Urgently*) You little fool! You will get punishment for not working! Come! (*The voices are louder now. Hans decides to get out quickly. He makes a strong, waving gesture at Louie as he goes out to indicate his displeasure. Outside the block the guards confront Hans. Angry voices come into the block. The next moment the door crashes open. Two guards haul a desperate and frightened looking Hans into the block. They literally throw him onto the floor. One guard raises his rifle butt to strike him but the second guard, a corporal, indicates: 'No. Wait'.*)

SECOND GUARD   (*Angrily*) Why are you here? (*First guard kicks Hans as he lies down, terror-stricken now. Neither guard has noticed Louie, who, seeing what is happening, has moved out of sight into his bunk as far as possible*)

FIRST GUARD   Speak up, you Polish pig! Why aren't you at your place of work?

HANS   (*Pleading*) I'm sick. (*First guard, another kick*)

SECOND GUARD   (*Sadistically*) You'll be sicker still when we tie you to a punishment post. A few days hanging like a parrot will stretch your arms out of your armpits till they are as loose as jelly.

HANS   (*Whimpering*) Please, please, I'll go to work right now.

FIRST GUARD   (*Sternly*) You're supposed to follow the rules, Kapo, not break them.

HANS   (*Grovelling*) Yes, yes, you are right. I'm sorry. I'm sorry.

SECOND GUARD   Get up! (*As Hans begins to rise, Louie sneezes loudly. The two guards look in the direction of the sound. They leave Hans and walk cautiously to the far end of the row of bunks (stage left corner). Hans remains standing, mutely terrified, sharing Louie's unfortunate discovery*)

FIRST GUARD   (*Discovering Louie, shouts*) Raus! Raus! Come on get out of your bunk! (*Louie scrambles out. Second guard grabs Louie by the ear, drags him over to Hans*)

SECOND GUARD   (*Laughing*) Two Jews to hang up like parrots today. (*Hans glares at Louie . . .All your fault for not listening to me*)

LOUIE   (*Rubbing his released ear*) My feet are sore. (*The two guards burst out laughing*)

FIRST GUARD   (*Sarcastically*) Shame. Maybe we can help you.

LOUIE   (*Naively*) You can?

SECOND GUARD   (*Playing along*) Sure. (*Indicates*) Here lie down and lift your feet up. (*Louie obeys, lies down on his back and raises his feet. First guard takes a firm grip on one foot. The second guard removes a box of matches from his top pocket, strikes a match, moves the lighted match downwards to Louie's foot now being kept in a firm grip. Hans watches helplessly at the coming torture.*) Guaranteed to cure sore feet. (*Just as the guard is about to burn Louie's foot, the door opens and Steiner enters. His face takes on a look of disgust and anger.*)

STEINER   (*Angrily*) What's going on here? (*Second guard snuffs out the match. First guard drops Louie's foot. By the tone of Steiner's voice, they realise he is not going to condone their sadism.*)

FIRST GUARD   We were having a bit of fun, Lieutenant. (*Defensively*) These Jews were larking off work.

STEINER   (*Not impressed*) Don't you have better things to do than play games with Jews? (*The guards are somewhat surprised at Steiner's attitude, but it is common knowledge that he does not display the Jew-hating attitude as openly as the other officers.*)

SECOND GUARD   Shall we take them to the punishment corporal?

STEINER   (*Firmly*) No. Leave them with me. (*Guards look at him puzzled. Steiner changes his mind*). Leave the boy. Take the Kapo.

SECOND GUARD   (*Cocky, pointing at Louie*) He should be punished too. Both were not at roll call.

STEINER   (*Forcefully*) Are you questioning my orders, corporal? (*The First guard gives the second guard's sleeve a tug, a 'come on, cool it', tug. Second guard realises he's gone far enough, although he is clearly not in agreement with Steiner*)

SECOND GUARD   (*Surly*) Very well, Lieutenant, as you wish. (*First guard grabs Hans by his jacket collar, half drags him out. Second guard looks over at Steiner and Louie with a mixture of suspicion and contempt. He reluctantly goes and shuts the door louder than usual.*)

LOUIE   (*Worried look, very concerned*) What is going to happen to Hans?

STEINER   He will be punished. A Kapo knows the rules.

LOUIE   (*Upset*) But it's my fault. He came to call me. My feet are sore. I was sleeping. He came back for me.

STEINER   (*Gently, like a father*) Let me see. Show me your feet. (*Louie holds up a foot for Steiner to see*) Yes, it looks sore. Have you been to the infirmary?

LOUIE   (*Like a child feeling guilty*) No.

STEINER   Come. I will take you there.

LOUIE   (*Anxiously*) Can't you stop Hans from being punished? He was only thinking of me. Hans cares for me. (*Sadly*) I don't want him hurt. (*Pleading*) Please . . .!

STEINER   I'll see what I can do. He won't be punished until tomorrow morning. There's enough time to stop it.

LOUIE   (*Pleased*) Promise?

STEINER   Yes. Come now, let me take you to the infirmary. (*As they are about to leave, the door opens and Kramer enters followed by an SS corporal. Kramer quickly takes in Steiner and Louie, but is unsure of what is going on.*)

KRAMER   (*Smiles, fakes surprise*) Ah . . . Lieutenant Steiner. We meet unexpectedly. (*Looking over Louie*) I see you have that troublesome little French Jew with you. He's not at work either. Do you wish me to take him off your hands?

STEINER   I was taking him to the infirmary. He is unable to work as he has difficulty in walking. His feet require treatment.

KRAMER   (*Makes a face, totally unsympathetic*) Jews are all

alike. Always trying to get out of things. Always
conniving. (*After giving Louie a contemptuous look*)
May I talk with you Herr Steiner? (*Quickly*) Not
what we discussed the other day, something else.

STEINER (*Reluctant*) Is it important?

KRAMER I think so.

STEINER Very well. Let me take this boy to the infirmary
first.

KRAMER (*Indicating*) Corporal Kellerman here can take him
whilst we talk. (*Steiner sizes up the corporal. Satisfied
that he seems a bit above the usual sadists, he agrees*)

STEINER (*To corporal*) Make sure you see that he receives
treatment. (*The corporal nods, takes Louie by the
arm, leads him out. Louie glances back at Steiner with
a 'thank you' look. Pause.*)

KRAMER (*Sighs wearily*) Sometimes I wish the war was over.
Everyday it's Jews, Jews, Jews. Why are there so
many Jews in the world? (*He sighs again.*)

STEINER What do you wish to discuss that is important?
(*Kramer removes a pack of cigarettes and a box of
matches.*)

KRAMER May I smoke?

STEINER Go ahead. (*Kramer offers the pack to Steiner*) Not
now, thanks. (*Kramer puts the pack back into his
pocket, lights up, puts the matches back in his pocket.*)

KRAMER (*Blowing out smoke*) Yesterday, the Kommandant
held a meeting. I overheard Möller. Some other
officers talking. Möller was complaining that you
get special treatment because you were excused
from attending. He was also complaining that

75

Captain Kleinsmidt had told him he was to report to your unit. He isn't happy about it.

STEINER (*A bit suspicious*) Why are you telling me this? What exactly are you getting at Kramer? (*Pause. Kramer smokes leisurely, takes his time to answer*).

KRAMER (*Bluntly*) There is talk that you are soft on Jews.

STEINER (*Annoyed*) So? Is that such a crime?

KRAMER (*Shrugs, blows a smoke ring*) In Auschwitz . . . yes. (*Grinds out the cigarette under his heel*)

STEINER (*Sarcastically*) So what do they, these so-called fellow officers, want me to do about it?

KRAMER (*Looks at him searchingly a moment*) They know you have been given permission to go to Berlin. They are worried that you might talk about our operations here. (*Pause*)

STEINER (*With a bit of bravado, but still taking it seriously*) What if I do? (*Pause*)

KRAMER Outsiders won't understand.

STEINER (*Puzzled*) Outsiders?

KRAMER (*Shrugs*) You know. Civilians. Other military outfits. You should know; you were in the Einsatzgruppen.

STEINER (*Sharply*) Why bring that up?

KRAMER (*Raising a defensive hand*) Just curious, that's all. Just curious why a man who served with the Einsatzgruppen comes to Auschwitz and is seen as being soft on Jews. Why the change? I mean, with respect, the Einsatzgruppen take nerves of steel and a steady hand.

STEINER   (*Coldly*) You're overreaching yourself. My past is
for me to live with. Thank you for the informa-
tion concerning Möller. However, to be frank,
I don't give a damn. Is that all now, Kramer?

KRAMER   (*Now trying to be friendly*) I have overstepped the
mark. I know I am out of line. No disrespect.
I come as a friend. You treated me decently
over my stupid behaviour at Kommandant
Hoess's house. I was thinking perhaps you
wanted to talk.

STEINER   (*Frowning*) Of . . . of what? (*Very slight pause*)

KRAMER   (*With some sympathy*) Look. This boy. This French
boy. I'm not blind. You like him. I can see that.

STEINER   (*Irritably*) Now we go into something else. First,
the talk about my softness with Jews, then the
Einsatzgruppen, now the French boy. What next
Kramer?

KRAMER   (*Shrugs*) I just thought you wanted to talk. I can
see you are discontented, unhappy.

STEINER   (*Brushing aside Kramer's invitation*) Some other
time. (*Then, looking distant, lost in thought somewhere, with feeling*) It's a long story, Kramer. (*Pause*)

KRAMER   (*Pressing*) You need a favour – ask – any time.

STEINER   (*Decently*) Kramer, you don't owe me anything.
Forget about trying to repay me. What I did for
you I would do for any soldier. Do we now
understand one another?

KRAMER   (*Slightly hurt*) As you wish, Herr Lieutenant. Good
day. (*Kramer salutes, exits*).

STEINER   (*Comes to front of stage. He seems far away in his thoughts, with great feeling)* Fritz . . .will you never leave me . . . WHY . . . WHY . . . WHY . . .? Why did I leave you to drown in those layers of cold, icy water? Was it because of our love, our devotion to one another? . . . Is my suffering never to end? (*The shunting of trains, whistles, dogs barking, the cries of children are heard in the distance. Slowly the light fades and the music of 'Wien, Wien, nur Du Allein', drifts in.*)

Light rises in the block. It is late evening, nearing eight o'clock. An inmate is sitting on one of the box chairs. His face is new, a new arrival assigned to Block A77. He has Louie's shoes and is examining them carefully. Voices are heard, then heavy footsteps approaching. He looks up, but continues to admire the shoes. Presently the door opens and the inmates, again exhausted from a twelve-hour day, shuffle in. The last inmate in is Louie. He stops, aghast that his shoes are in the hands of someone else. He rushes over to the startled inmate and grabs the shoes.

LOUIE   (*Sharply*) Hell, what are you doing with my shoes?

INMATE   (*Jumping up*) Your shoes?

LOUIE   (*Furious*) You leave my shoes alone! (*Grabs them*)

INMATE   (*Timidly*) I did not know they belonged to any-one. (*Indicating*) I found them in the bunk over there. (*Other inmates ignore what is happening, climb into their bunks*)

LOUIE   (*Calming down*) You are new here. I haven't seen you before. (*He hugs his shoes*)

INMATE   (*Relieved*) Yes. My name is Willem Brukmann. And yours?

LOUIE   (*Friendly*) Louie Mausalt.

INMATE   French?

Shoes

LOUIE   Yes. And you?

INMATE   Dutch. From Holland

LOUIE   (*Ingenuously*) Why do you come so far?

INMATE   (*Amused*) I had no choice. The Germans caught me selling cheese on the black market and put me on a train with Jews to come here to Auschwitz.

LOUIE   (*Curious*) You are a cheesmaker?

INMATE   No, a shoemaker.

LOUIE   (*Excitedly*) A shoemaker! A real shoemaker?

INMATE   (*Solemnly*) In Amsterdam I had my own shop until the Germans came and closed me down.

LOUIE   (*Frowning*) Why?

INMATE   (*Slowly explaining*) They thought I was a Jew. When I tried to show them my papers, my birth certificate, they tore it up. You are a Jew bastard, they said, and smashed up my shop. Just like that. To survive, I smuggled cheese from the farms to help my starving family. But one night I was unlucky. I broke the curfew and a patrol caught me. They shot all my family.

LOUIE   (*Quietly*) I'm sorry for you.

INMATE   (*Shrugs*) That's the story of my life. Living with the shadows. Never any sunshine. (*Pause*)

LOUIE   (*Warmly*) You can look at my shoes now if you want to. (*Louie hands over the shoes to Brukmann. Louie pulls over his box chair next to the other chair. They sit down close together.*)

INMATE   (*Checking over the shoes, bending them*) Hmmm . . .

real leather. Very good quality. Must have cost a lot of money. Good shoes for walking.

LOUIE (*Very interested*) Real leather. How can you tell?

INMATE (*Demonstrates*) See how soft they are. You can bend them over easily. Cheap shoes would just break in half. (*Hands shoes back to Louie*)

LOUIE (*Delighted*) Real leather. (*Smells them lovingly*)

INMATE The best. (*Louie puts shoes on his lap*)

LOUIE (*Impressed*) You know a lot about shoes.

INMATE (Modestly) I suppose so. After twenty-five years fixing up shoes, I guess I know a little more than some people. (*Curiously*) Where did you get these shoes?

LOUIE (*Warming to Brukmann, companionably*) It's a funny story. Do you want me to tell you?

INMATE (*Now friendly*) If you like. Such nice shoes must have a story to be in a place like this.

LOUIE (*Slowly making himself comfortable*) You see I have a friend, Hans. He is always making promises to me, but he can never keep them. One day he promises he'll get me chicken, another day, something else. Always, just promises and nothing happens. Look at my feet. (*He holds up a foot for Brukmann to see. Brukmann looks, frowns, nods in sympathy*) Swollen from all the standing. (*Very short pause*) Last week comes a new German Officer. Very nice man. He likes me. Tells me that I remind him of his friend who drowned. He sees my old boots and I tell him my feet are very sore from standing in front of my machine at the factory at Monowitz all day. Then one day, I think it was the next day, he comes to the factory. Again we talk. The supervisor says nothing. The SS can do what they like. So he asks me again, 'how's your feet Louie?' I say 'very sore'. So he says he will go to Canada, – that's the name of the warehouse where Hans, my friend, works – and he will look for a pair of shoes. After he goes, I think, ag, it's all talk, all promises, just like Hans. Maybe he just wants to be nice to me so that he can make love to me the way Hans does. But no, what happens? The next night. Yes, yes, two nights ago, I come back here to the block and a guard comes in and says he has a parcel for me. It was these shoes. Can you believe it? (*Excitedly*) Can you believe it? The SS sending me, Louie Mausalt, a Jew from Paris, shoes! Huh, can you believe it? (*Inmate shrugs, makes a face*)

INMATE (*Philosophically*) Well, as you said, the SS can do anything they want.

LOUIE (*Wondering*) Yes, even here in Auschwitz. (*Pause*)

INMATE (*Lifting a shoe from Louie's lap*) So they fit you? They look too big for your small feet. Even swollen, you have small feet. Size seven. Maybe seven and a half. But not bigger. (*Looks inside shoe for size, doesn't find any, estimates with his fingers*). I reckon these are nine. Maybe nine and a half. Too big for you. (*Louie suspicious, takes the shoe away from Brukmann. Puts shoes together, tucks them into his lap, places his hands protectively over them*)

LOUIE (*Cooling off his friendliness*) It's time to get some rest now. (*Pause. Louie begins to move away from Brukmann. Brukmann looks very lonely*)

INMATE (*Worried*) Don't we get food?

LOUIE (*Getting up*) Not tonight. We had food at the factory. We do not get food more than once per day.

INMATE (*Anxiously*) What do I eat? I haven't had food for two days?

LOUIE You have to ask the Kapo.

INMATE (*Looking around*) Who is he?

LOUIE He's not here. The SS took him away to the punishment block and he has not come back.

INMATE (*Terrified*) Punishment block?

LOUIE (*Matter-of-factly*) They whip you, or if you are very bad, hang you from a pole with your feet off the ground and your hands tied behind you back for a few days.

INMATE (*Appalled*) What monsters! (*Louie wipes his shoes*)

LOUIE (*Yearningly*) I wish I had some polish for my shoes.

INMATE Which is my bunk?

LOUIE (*Indicating*) Those near the door are empty. The bunk where you found the shoes is my bunk. The bunk above me is for Hans, my friend.

INMATE Well, I guess that's it then. (*He goes to his bunk. As he goes, the door opens and Hans rushes in, sees Louie, puts his arms around him, bear-hugs him. Louie struggles to breathe, shoes drop from his grasp.*)

HANS (*Gushing emotionally*) Louie! Louie! Louie! My

little angel! My little darling! (*Louie manages to break free, holds Hans away by pushing his shoulders*)

LOUIE (*Recovering*) Hans. I thought . . . (*Hans puts a finger tenderly on Louie's lips*)

HANS (*Secretively*) Sssshhh . . .I don't want them (*Indicating*) to hear. (*In a lower voice*) They didn't punish me, Louie. They let me go.

LOUIE (*In a low voice, pleased*) It was because of Captain Steiner. He's a good man. (*Hans is not happy at the mention of Steiner, even though it is apparent that it was due to Steiner's actions that he has been freed.*)

HANS (*Jealous*) He's still an SS pig! (*Takes Louie's arms*)

LOUIE (*Defensively*) He helped you. You should be happy.

HANS (*Smirkingly*) Happy – in this shithole? Not even a lunatic can be happy here. (*Pause*)

LOUIE You're back, Hans, that's enough to be happy about. (*Hans puts his arms around Louie's waist, draws him closer, kisses him tenderly*)

HANS (*Horny*) Come, my little angel. (*Hans leads Louie by the hand to Louie's bunk. The light begins to fade. Hans and Louie climb into the bunk together. As darkness envelops the stage, we hear the now familiar shunting and movement of trains. A whistle blows, dogs bark. Voices far off in the distance. Dogs bark louder. The haunting cries of children. A shaft of light falls on the now abandoned pair of shoes, cutting through the now totally enveloping darkness highlighting them.*)

Early morning. Light has risen in the block. The inmates have gone to their places of work. Voices off are heard, then the sound of heavy footsteps. The half-door is flung open, young Möller enters accompanied by Kramer. Möller walks up and down examining the bedding etc. He views everything with distaste and arrogance. Kramer stands with his hands behind his back. Möller wipes his hands on his handkerchief, vigorously intent on doing away with any germs.

MÖLLER   (*Scowling*) This place is a pigsty! Full of lice. Doesn't Steiner know these are unacceptable standards?

KRAMER   (*Indulgently*) No worse than everywhere else (*Checks some mattresses himself, smells.*). This block was fumigated a few days ago. Any lice would be eradicated by now.

MÖLLER   (*Full of youthful cocksureness*) I disagree, Sergeant Kramer. This place is enough to give me a case of durchfall (diarrhoea). Surely you can see for yourself it is filthy? (*With an edge of sarcasm*) You're not a schreibstube (office worker), Sergeant Kramer. Your own intelligence can tell you that this block and all the other blocks under Steiner's control are below acceptable standards. (*Kramer realises that Möller is out to 'rubbish' Steiner. At the same time he is not willing to 'buck' Möller, who outranks him*)

KRAMER   (*Diplomatically*) May I suggest, Acting Lieutenant Möller, that you take it up with Lieutenant Steiner personally?

MÖLLER   (*Turns on him sharply*) Good idea, Sergeant. (*Just then Steiner enters through the open door. He has heard the last part of the conversation*)

STEINER   (*Cool*) You have a problem, Lieutenant Möller?

MÖLLER   (*Snottily*) Acting Lieutenant.

STEINER   (*With forced courtesy*) Very well, Acting Lieutenant

Möller. So you have a problem? (*Kramer moves away*)

MÖLLER (*Officiously*) This block and all the other blocks are infested with lice. I have personally checked and satisfied myself that the required standards of hygiene are not being met. Kommandant Hoess requested me to ensure that our standards are always maintained. Since being posted to your command from the showers, I took it as my first duty to do an inspection. I find a most unsatisfactory situation.

STEINER (*Cynically*) Worse than the showers, hey? Gassing is cleaner? (*Very short pause. Möller is straining at the bit. He wrestles with his boiling emotions, having now been stung by Steiner. Steiner waits for his reaction*)

MÖLLER (*With suppressed anger*) We do not use the term gassing, Herr Steiner. If you were familiar with the rules, you would know that the correct term is 'treated appropriately'. By attending meetings, we learn about such things. (*Sarcastically*) Of course, some are lucky enough not to attend.

STEINER (*Firmly with a strong edge of sarcasm*) Thank you for enlightening me on some euphemisms I am apparently not conversant with. It seems that I shall have to attend all meetings in future. As a matter of fact, I shall enlist your help in future, by requesting you to provide me with a handwritten report of all the terminology required for my education in matters such as the Final Solution requires. You can go to your quarters right now and make a start. (*In the background, Kramer is taking great pleasure in seeing Möller being taken down a peg. Kramer grins widely, but unseen by Steiner and Möller. Möller realises he is out of line, tries hard to force a friendly smile.*)

MÖLLER (*Fawning*) Herr Steiner – Lieutenant Steiner, you have taken things up the wrong way. I mean no disrespect. It's just that I wish to serve your section of Auschwitz as best I can.

STEINER (*Not giving ground*) Well you have made a good start, Acting Lieutenant Möller. If it had not been for your sharp sense of duty, no doubt acquired by your commitment to the tasks at the showers, we would not have realised how below standard our blocks are in this section under my command. So really, I must be grateful to you. I wish, therefore, that before you write out all the terminology of the Final Solution lacking in my education, that you personally – and I emphasise – personally, take two guards, not inmates, and begin to fumigate all the blocks in my section. That is an order, Acting Lieutenant Möller. Understood?

MÖLLER (*Protesting*) But, Herr Steiner, with respect, what will the inmates think? What will the guards think, having to carry out such orders?

STEINER (*Rubbing it in*) Acting Lieutenant Möller, you attend meetings. That is your problem. A good SS officer always finds a solution, does he not? Good day, Lieutenant. Carry out your first orders under my command. (*Their eyes meet briefly*)

MÖLLER (*Stiffly*) Very well, Herr Lieutenant Steiner. (*He

86

clicks his heels sharply, marches out with a sulky expression. Kramer comes over to Steiner with a wry smile)

KRAMER *(Contemptiously)* Brainwashed. A walking robot. A machine with no feelings whatsoever.

STEINER *(Surprised)* Do I hear you correctly?

KRAMER *(Explaining)* Coming from me, such a comment does somewhat confuse you. It confuses me too. *(Very slight pause).* But I stopped trying to justify what we are doing here a long time ago. I no longer stop to consider what we are doing or what is being done. Of course, like Möller, my moral sense is dulled by my job conditioning and diminished further by the mechanics of the task in hand. *(He sighs heavily)* But, I, like you, like everyone, like Möller, am still a human being, not so? *(Steiner takes out cigarettes and matches, lights up, hands matches and cigarettes to Kramer who lights up. They smoke).*

STEINER *(Considering Kramer)* You surprise me, yes, Kramer. Underneath that uniform, you're quite a philosopher.

KRAMER *(Jokingly)* And a peeping tom, to say nothing of the rest of it.

STEINER *(Seriously)* Seriously though, Kramer, we can't fool ourselves that we can simply bury our concience along with the ashes of the crematoriums. Of course, we have hundreds of different personalities working amongst us. If we did not have the Möllers and the brainless, the morons, the guards, those Special Kommandos and Kapos,

Auschwitz would simply grind to a halt. The
sheer size of it all, Kramer, that's what I find
difficult to come to terms with. Sometimes I wake
up in the night, cold, covered with sweat, unable
to sleep again, and then I lie awake and think to
myself it has to end some day – the war – and
then – what about Auschwitz? What will become
of it . . . and us? (*Pause*)

KRAMER We'll close it up. Like you close up a factory.
And we'll go home. You to your music, me to
my dreams. My girl in Munich, my farm . . .
(*Very slight pause*)

STEINER And Auschwitz?

KRAMER Just bulldoze it all away.

STEINER (*Cynically*) As simple as that?

KRAMER (*Insensitively*) Why not? It will make a good vegetable garden. All that Jewish ash. Good fertilizer. (*Jokes*) Maybe I should farm here, not
outside Munich. No need to buy any fertilizer,
jah? (*Laughs, then slight pause*)

STEINER (*Changing the subject*) I leave for Berlin tomorrow.

KRAMER Yes, I've heard. (*Steiner stubbs out his cigarette.*)

STEINER (*After a pause*) Can I ask a favour of you?

KRAMER (*Eagerly*) Of course. (*Stubbs cigarette out.*)

STEINER The French boy. Keep an eye on him. I promised
I would move him to Hoess's house. (*Kramer gives
Steiner a quizzical look*) I know it sounds odd to
you, asking a favour for a Jew. Please don't ask
me to explain. Will you do it? (*Pause*)

KRAMER (*Considering*) Yes.

STEINER I will pay you a sum of money towards your farm.

KRAMER (*Somewhat offended*) No. No, there's no need for that. It's a simple task you ask of me. (*Worried*) As long as it's within my control.

STEINER What do you mean?

KRAMER Well, whilst you are in Berlin, Möller will be in charge. Who knows what that upstart will do? Maybe he will send everybody to the showers. You know, he likes that kind of thing.

STEINER Try to look after him.

KRAMER Very well.

STEINER Thank you. (*Steiner looks at his watch*) It's time for inspection. Kleinsmidt is a fanatic for being on time. Excuse me, Kramer, I must hurry. (*He turns to leave*)

KRAMER (*Anxiously*) One thing before you go. (*Steiner turns back*)

STEINER Yes?

KRAMER (*With concern*) If anything happens to the boy whilst you are in Berlin, you must not blame me for it. (*Their eyes meet*)

STEINER (*Quietly*) I understand.

KRAMER Thank you. (*Steiner exits quickly. Kramer is left thinking. He is troubled by Steiner's request, but he feels that he owes him a favour in return for having heard him out over the incident at Hoess's house. He idles a bit longer, walks along the bunks. His eye catches something. He stops, reaches for something in Louie's bunk. He pulls out Louie's shoes. He examines them curiously, puts them down on the floor, measures his boots against them. Finding that they are too small, he tosses them back into the bunk. As he is about to leave, the Dutchman, Brukmann enters. He carries a pail of soapy water and a mop. Seeing Kramer, he gives a frightened start. Kramer sizes him up.)* Why are you here?

BRUKMANN *(Nervously)* The young blond Lieutenant Möller took me out from kitchen duties peeling potatoes and told me to clean the floor here in block A77.

KRAMER *(Officiously)* Do you live in this block?

BRUKMANN *(Frightened)* Yes.

KRAMER *(Indicating)* Whose shoes are those? Over there?

BRUKMANN *(Stuttering)* The . . . French . . . French . . . boy . . . Louie . . . Louie Mausalt . . . *(His eyes are wide, fear stricken)*

KRAMER Hmmm – did he steal them?

BRUKMANN *(Stuttering)* I – I – don't know. He said, he said, an SS Lieuten . . . *(He realises he is talking about a German officer, breaks off in fear.)*

KRAMER *(Coaxing)* Come now. I'm not going to do anything to you. All I am asking is an ordinary question. *(But Brukmann is tongue-tied with fear. Realising this, Kramer takes on a much softer tone now)* Did he mention the name Steiner? Lieutenant Steiner? *(Brukmann swallows hard. He is shaking)*

BRUKMANN *(Nodding)* I think so. *(Kramer smiles)*

KRAMER *(In a normal tone of voice now and with a more relaxed manner)* Good. Now tell me. Why doesn't he wear his shoes? Such nice shoes should be worn. (*Sarcastically*) Why, the person who went up the chimney would be sad. (*Indicates*) Up there in heaven, if his beautiful shoes were not being worn down here on earth.

BRUKMANN (*A little more composed now*) He has sore feet but he wears them at night. I've seen him wear them at night after we've all gone to bed. He gets out of his bunk, puts on the shoes and walks up and down. But those shoes are too big for him. I've told him but he won't listen to me.

KRAMER (*Sarcastic again. Drops his soft manner*) Who are you . . . his father?

BRUKMANN (*Sheepishly*) No, I'm a shoemaker.

KRAMER (*Unimpressed*) Ag so! (*Very slight pause, then sarcastically again*) Well now, you're no longer a shoemaker, but a cleaner. Get to work! (*Brukmann begins to mop the floor furiously. Kramer watches for a moment, then exits. As the door shuts, Brukmann stops his mopping task, goes over to Louie's bunk and removes the shoes. He carries the shoes carefully and goes over to one of the box chairs, sits down, removes his own huge boots, tries on Louie's shoes. They seem to fit. He gets up, walks around, relishing the feel of such a fine pair of soft, leather shoes. Off stage, voices are heard approaching. He listens, his heart going fast now. Realising the voices are nearer now, he rushes over to Louie's bunk, puts back the shoes under the mattress, rushes to where he left his mop, takes it up again, begins to mop. The door suddenly crashes open and an SS guard enters. He pauses momentarily and watches Brukmann mopping the floor. Satisfied that the work is being done as ordered by Möller, exits. The door shuts. Brukmann stops mopping, puts out his tongue, follows it with an 'up yours' sign, then continues mopping. The shunting of trains is heard followed by trains getting up steam, then whistles, then a cacophony of voices. Brukmann stops mopping, listens. He shakes his head in sympathy.)*

The light fades into darkness. Then slowly light rises sharply over Hoess's desk. Kleinsmidt is standing next to the desk. It appears he is waiting for someone as he glances at his watch intermittently. A few moments later the door opens and young Möller walks in quickly. They exchange salutes. It is late afternoon.

MÖLLER (*A bit breathlessly,*) My apologies, Captain Kleinsmidt. Unfortunately I was detained longer than expected at the revier. One of my men injured himself.

KLEINSMIDT (*Testily*) I do not like to be kept waiting, Lieutenant Möller. My responsibilities are such that I do not want my time taken up by waiting around.

MÖLLER (*Fervently apologetical now*) I'm sorry. It will not happen again. (*Very slight pause*)

KLEINSMIDT Good. Now down to business. Do you wish to sit? (*Indicates*)

MÖLLER (*Stiffly*) Thank you, no. I prefer to stand. (*Kleinsmidt gives him a long look*)

KLEINSMIDT Very well, as you wish. (*He places his hands together and rubs them for a moment whilst he collects his thoughts. Möller now stands dutifully with his hands behind his back awaiting orders*) As you know,

Kommandant Hoess is indisposed with the 'flu for a few days. However, our duties do not fall away because of it and we must continue to keep up the good work we are doing for the Fatherland. (*Pause. He continues slowly*) This morning we were notified that fifty thousand Jews are to be sent to Auschwitz from Holland shortly. At our last meeting you made mention of the fact to Herr Kommandant Hoess that our facilities were inadequate. I must agree with you, Möller, that at times they are. But it is not a question really of facilities, Möller, but of poor logistic engineering. Now, this morning's notification was typical of what I am talking about. Out of the blue, fifty thousand Jews are on the way. (*Very slight pause again*) And why? Why to Auschwitz and not to the other centres? (*Very slight pause*) I'll tell you why, Möller. Because we run a very efficient operation here and the Reichsführer, Herr Himmler, knows it. That's why, Möller, all the trains head this way. (*He pauses to pour a glass of water from a tumbler on Hoess's desk. He sips.*) Ahh. To continue. So we now have a problem. A problem of accomodation. (*Very slight pause*) And how do we solve it, Möller? (*Their eyes meet. Kleinsmidt is waiting for an answer the way a schoolmaster waits for an answer from a pupil*)

MÖLLER (*Confidently*) We must increase our 'appropriate treatment'. Clear one hundred blocks immediately.

KLEINSMIDT (*Impressed*) Immediately. Good, that's what I like to hear, Möller. No dilly-dallying. (*Very slight*

pause) Now where do you propose we start?
(*Möller now relaxes a bit, his self confidence encouraged
by Kleinsmidt to the point of cockiness*).

MÖLLER   (*Smugly*) Easy. We start with Lieutenant Steiner's
section and work our way systematically over one
hundred blocks. I can have my men ready within
one hour. (*Pause*)

KLEINSMIDT   (*Weighing up, considering*) Ja gut. But Steiner's
section are all recently trained workers for the
Monowitz factories. We cannot allow production
to be affected. Not even for one day.

MÖLLER   (*Ingratiatingly*) With respect, Captain Kleinsmidt,
I have only just yesterday done an inspection of
Lieutenant Steiner's section at his request. And I
found that ninety per cent of those Monowitz
workers are either sick or too old. We can very
easily replace them from the fifty thousand expected soon from Holland. I am sure Lieutenant
Steiner will be only too pleased to get a new
compliment of younger, stronger workers. I've
heard that the Dutch are good workers. (*Pause*)

KLEINSMIDT   (*Considering*) What if the Hollanders are all old
or women and children?

MÖLLER   (*Confidently*) Not fifty thousand, surely! With respect, Herr Captain Kleinsmidt, our statistics
show that at least some twenty per cent can be
efficiently utilised.

KLEINSMIDT   (*Rolling his lips, satisfied*) I see you do your home-
work, Möller. Very well, go ahead. (*Möller beams*)
But, just one detail, Möller (*Möller pays extra
attention*) We do not want panic to spread. Such

a large operation, clearing one hundred blocks, requires good organisation, good management. I suggest you start after the people to be treated have finished their evening meal. Use a small group of soldiers. One or two blocks at a time. Let Feldwebel Sergeant Kramer be involved. He knows the ropes pretty well. Good, that will be all.

MÖLLER (*Keenly*) You can count on me, Captain. The sections will all be swept clean by midnight. (*Kleinsmidt nods and gives a thin smile.*)

KLEINSMIDT Heil Hitler! (*They exchange salutes*)

MÖLLER Heil Hitler! (*He goes*)

KLEINSMIDT (*Moves over to telephone, dials a number, barks as he sits down in Hoess's chair*) Get me Headquarters, Amsterdam. Colonel Derrick Bronmann, urgently. (*He waits for the connection. Sips more water. Slight pause. The connection comes through*) Bronmann? Kleinsmidt. Ja gut. Danke. You can go ahead. Send as many Jews as you like. (*Listens*) Ja gut. (*Laughs*) Labour utilization. Ja, danke. Gut. (*Listens*) Gut. Aufwiedersehen. (*Slowly, thoughtfully, replaces phone. Sips water. Then exits. The light fades slowly. Loud shunting of trains.*)

Light rises in the Block. It is very late afternoon, but the inmates have not as yet returned to the block from their various jobs. The door opens and Kramer enters followed by two SS guards. The last guard to enter peers out, checks that all is clear, and shuts the door.

KRAMER (*Taking out a pack of cigarettes and offering them*) Here, let's have a smoke.

GUARDS (*Taking cigarettes*) Danke. (*Kramer takes out a box of matches, lights up cigarettes all round. Pause as they smoke.*)

KRAMER (*Speaking easily with no tension, friendly, addresses each guard in turn, by name*) Rudi. Werner. We've been together a long time. First the front, now here. (*Very slight pause*) Ja, we've had some good times and some bad times together. (*Reminiscing*) Remember the time we laid those Polish whores? (*The guards laugh, Kramer joins in*) And how we all got the swollen balls for our trouble? (*Yearningly*) I sometimes wish those days were back. (*Pause. They smoke*) Now, let's talk quickly before we have to get back for Möller's orders. Let me fill you in. We're going to clear one hundred blocks tonight. (*The SS guards exchange glances*) Starting right here with this block. (*Guards look on very attentively*) Möller, I know, will let me handle Lieutenant Steiner's section, and in turn I will assign my men to each block to be cleared. Now, I am going to assign you two to this block. Clear? (*The two guards nod*) What I want you to do is this. (*Very slight pause as they let their eyes meet Kramer's intently*) I want you to clear this block completely (*He pauses*). Completely, but with one exception. One inmate must be allowed to remain behind. (*The guards frown, puzzled looks*). I know it sounds out of line. Unfortunately, I can't explain the reasons now. Later in the recreation room, when this is all over, I'll tell you why over a few beers. Understood? (*Pause. They continue to smoke*).

FIRST GUARD   Jews all look alike. How will Rudi and I know which Jew is not to go?

KRAMER   (*Explaining*) He'll be wearing shoes, not boots.

SECOND GUARD   (*Amused*) Himmel! What next? Now we have Jews wearing shoes, not boots. (*Voices, footsteps are heard approaching. Kramer and the guards exchange quick glances. Kramer indicates for them to go to the door, check. First guard goes, cautiously opens door, peeps out. He turns back, mouths 'Kleinsmidt.' Quickly shuts door, quickly returns to Kramer's position. They stub out cigarettes.*)

KRAMER   (*Urgently. Guards now nervous, don't pay too much attention.*) Got it? (*They nod to Kramer.*) Right. Be careful. Just leave him behind. I'll see to the rest. Don't discuss this with . . . (*His voice trails off as the door opens and Kleinsmidt enters. He walks over to the group. They exchange salutes*)

KLEINSMIDT   (*Suspicious*) A meeting? (*Looks guards up and down*)

KRAMER   (*Quickly*) Just a briefing, Herr Captain Kleinsmidt. (*Kleinsmidt sniffs the air. He knows they have been smoking, but decides to let it go.*)

KLEINSMIDT   (*Making a face*) Stuffy in here. (*Very slight pause*) Well, dismiss your men, Kramer, I want a talk with you. (*Kramer indicates to the guards they can go. They salute and leave. Kleinsmidt waves the air deliberately.*) Smoking is bad for you. On top of that, the air here is full of smoke. Do you want your lungs to rot?

KRAMER   (*Sheepishly*) No, Captain.

KLEINSMIDT   You know about our operation for tonight?

KRAMER   Yes.

KLEINSMIDT   (*Rubs his chin considering*) I'm worried about
Steiner not being here. Möller is a very keen
soldier, but young and inexperienced. (*Very slight
pause*) I want you to stay out of the block-clearing
operation. Leave that to Möller. (*Very slight pause*).
Of course you must assign your men. But I want
you at the trucks. You've been through all this
before. Möller hasn't. Understood? (*Kramer nods*)

KRAMER   (*Attentively*) Understood, mein Kapitein.

KLEINSMIDT   Gut. (*He sniffs the air again. They exchange salutes,
he goes. Kramer visibly relaxes, lets out a sigh, wipes
his brow. He is thinking, 'Thank God, I did not get
caught instructing the guards. Only smoking.'*)

KRAMER   (*To himself with relief. Addresses the audience*)
Steiner . . . now you and I are square. We are
even. I've saved your little Jewish boy. (*He shakes
out a cigarette, lights up, takes a deep draw, lets the
smoke out slowly as the tension drains from his body.
The loud shunting and coupling of trains is heard. The
light fades very slowly as Kramer goes.*)

*Light slowly rises. Hoess's office now converts to the living room of the Steiner
household in Berlin. The desk remains, but the chairs are replaced by two large
armchairs placed a fair distance apart and divided by a large coffee table. There is
a tray on the table with cups and saucers, a sugar bowl and a large silver coffee
pot. Light focuses in a circle over the two chairs and the table. All the rest of the
stage is in darkness. Steiner enters. He is dressed in a suit, collar and tie, crisp
white shirt, shiny black shoes, and carries a folded newspaper under his arm. He
could pass for a banker now in his civilian attire. He pours a cup of coffee, sits
down, opens up the newspaper, reads, pauses every now and then to sip his coffee,
which he leaves on the coffee table. A few moments pass, then Steiner Snr. enters.*

Shoes

He is rather stout, approaching seventy, scholarly looking, correctly dressed in a sombre suit, very German, formal and decided. He comes over to Steiner Jnr. He looks down at the tray.

STEINER SNR. No milk again. (*Steiner Jnr. looks up from his paper*)

STEINER JNR. That's all right, father. I'm fortunate to enjoy just good coffee. No milk doesn't matter. (*He smiles warmly*)

STEINER SNR. Real Brazilian.

STEINER JNR. I recognised the taste. Very good.

STEINER SNR. I'm glad you like it. (*He sighs tiredly, sits down*)

STEINER JNR. (*Putting aside his newspaper*) Nothing but propaganda. (*Steiner Snr. pours coffee for himself*)

STEINER SNR. (*Sips*) Ah. (*Rolling his lips pleasurably*) Helga makes good coffee. (*Sips with enjoyment*)

STEINER JNR. You do realise it's her day off?

STEINER SNR. (*Putting aside his coffee*) Ach. She only came in for a few hours to make our breakfast. The rest of the day she has to herself. Besides, she wanted to meet you. (*Pause, rather sadly, fondly recalling*) Your mother used to make such good coffee too. (*Very slight pause*) You know, the day of the air raid, the day she was killed, I actually said to her, 'My darling, you make beautiful coffee'. (*He closes his eyes, fondly remembering*) Such beautiful coffee. (*A fairly long pause*).

STEINER JNR. (*Gently*) Did you sleep well? (*Steiner Snr. opens his eyes. Alert again. Sips his coffee intermittently*)

STEINER SNR. (*Rubbing his temples*) I had a bad headache. All night I couldn't sleep.

99

STEINER JNR. (*With concern*) Can I get you something?

STEINER SNR. It's better now. (*Very slight pause*) It's those photographs you showed me.

STEINER JNR. I didn't mean to upset you father, but I felt you should know.

STEINER SNR. (*Puzzled*) How did you get them?

STEINER JNR. I took them secretly. It was very difficult to do. I had to be extremely careful. Had I been discovered, it could have had very serious consequences.

STEINER SNR. (*Uncomprehending*) I can't believe it. When we talked last night and you began to tell me about that place, Auschwitz, and took out those photographs, I felt that I was listening to fairy tales. Then the lights went out. Another air raid and we went to bed. But during the night I lay awake, my brain full of those terrible pictures. I couldn't sleep. I tried, but those pictures kept coming back. (*Very slight pause*) How can such things happen?

STEINER JNR. It happens father. People get carried away. Individually we condemn, but in a group we go along. After a while we accept and become insensitive to it all. It becomes an industrial exercise, no longer human, no longer flesh and blood. Just a function, impersonal, mechanical, bureaucratic. A sidestepping of everything moral. Just an ongoing focus on logistics and production. And all in the name of serving the Fatherland. (*Pause*)

STEINER SNR. (*Confused*) But how can Germans do such things?

Shoes

We who gave the world Goethe, Schiller, Beethoven, Handel . . .? (*He shakes his head*) I'm just an old man. I cannot believe such things exist in the world. War is war. But this – this killing of millions of people like a factory! No, no, I cannot believe it. I'm sorry.

STEINER JNR. It's true, father. Everything I have told you, everything I have shown you, is there, father, before my eyes. Every day I see what I have told you. (*Pause*)

STEINER SNR. (*Wearily, sadly*) And you . . . you are part of it? (*Very short pause*) Part of this bestial place?

STEINTER JNR. (*Softly*) Yes, father. (*Pause*)

STEINER SNR. (*Non-judgmental*) Can you get out of it? (*Very slight pause.*)

STEINER JNR. It's very difficult, father. Just to have these few days with you would not have happened if it had not been for the fact that my superiors know that you have very high connections. Regrettably, they are the sort of men who are driven by ambition and I confess I took advantage of it.

STEINER SNR. Well, thank God that you are here. Now we can do something about it.

STEINER JNR. What do you mean, father?

STEINER SNR. (*Firmly*) You must leave Auschwitz.

STEINER JNR. It's not possible. No officer – in fact no one, leaves Auschwitz easily.

STEINER SNR. (*Adamantly*) You must go and see Himmler. Tell him you want out. Tell him you need a change. Anything.

STEINER JNR.   (*Slowly, patiently*) Father, Himmler is the last one to speak to.

STEINER SNR.   Well then, Hitler. I will go with you. (*Starts getting up*) I will phone his secretary now and make an appointment to see him.

STEINER JNR.   Please sit down, father. (*Pause*) You know, father, I served in the Einsatzgruppen on the Russian front. An extermination squad . . .

STEINER SNR.   (*Confused*) But I thought . . . (*He looks sad*)

STEINER JNR.   (*Guiltily*) The reconnaissance? No, father, that was a lie. (*Very slight pause*)

STEINER SNR.   (*Shrugs*) In wartime, everybody has to tell a few lies.

STEINER JNR.   I volunteered father. I willingly went to Russia to kill people. (*Steiner Snr. bows his head*) You see, father, I belong in Auschwitz. There is no way out. (*Pause*)

STEINER SNR.   (*Wipes away a tear*) I understand. (*Pause, then heavily*) War is like that. People have to do things they wouldn't otherwise do. You had to do your duty. You are a soldier. A soldier has to obey orders. (*He lifts his head slowly*)

STEINER JNR.   No, father. I wanted to kill.

STEINER SNR.   (*Shocked*) But why?! (*Pause*)

STEINER JNR.   (*With emotion*) It was something inside me, father. Something that had to come out. Guilt. Anger. Pain . . .

STEINER SNR.   (*Gently*) Fritz? (*Their eyes meet.*)

STEINER JNR.   (*Sharply*) Fritz?! (*Very short pause*)

STEINER SNR.   (*Very gently*) I've known for a long time. (*Fairly long pause*) We can talk about it. If you want to talk about it. (*Pause*)

STEINER JNR.   How did you know? (*Pause*)

STEINER SNR.   Your diary.

STEINER JNR.   (*Puzzled*) But I tore it up.

STEINER SNR.   (*Slowly explaining*) I took it out of the dustbin and put it all together again, piece by piece. You see, when you left for the army, the day you left, the day you tore it up and we took you to the station, I came back and found it in pieces when I went to throw the rubbish out. I was afraid I would never see you again. So I – so I took it out, piece by piece, and put it all together again. I know it was a bad thing to do, to pry into someone's private thoughts, but I couldn't help myself. I had this fear, this fear . . . and the diary was all I would have left. (*Sadly*) Do you understand why? Why, why you have such a foolish father . . .? (*Pause*)

STEINER JNR.   (*With great feeling*) I understand, father. (*Pause*)

STEINER SNR.   (*Pathetically*) I'm a sorry excuse for a father. (*Pause*)

STEINER JNR.   (*Gently*) No, father. You're the best father one could ever wish for. (*Pause, then slowly and painfully*) I did not wish for Fritz to die father. I was a coward. I could not bring myself to help him. I – I just don't know, father, why I couldn't move. I lied, father. All these years, I've lived a lie. (*Pause*) And all the time, father, you knew the truth. The truth I wrote in my diary. (*Pause*)

And – and all these years you never said you knew I was a coward. (*Pause*)

STEINER SNR.   (*Gently*) You are my son. You made a mistake. I know the heavy burden you bear. I know the pain and anger inside. It happened. Nothing can change what happened. Life must go on. (*Pause*)

STEINER JNR.   (*Quietly*) Do you forgive me, father? (*Pause*)

STEINER SNR.   (*With compassion*) A father's heart is there to forgive. I forgave you long ago. (*Pause. Steiner Jnr. wipes an eye, composes himself, looks lovingly at his father*)

STEINER JNR.   (*Softly*) Thank you, father. (*An awkward silence follows. Then Steiner Snr. places his hand on the coffee urn*) It's still hot. More coffee? (*Steiner Jnr. moves forward. Their eyes meet. Warmth and understanding.*)

STEINER JNR.   (*Quietly*) May I have my diary back, father? (*Steiner Snr. smiles with affection at his son; he nods. The light very slowly fades as Steiner Snr. pours more coffee. Then Steiner Snr. rises and prepares to go.*)

STEINER SNR.   I will fetch the diary. (*He goes. The light now fades rapidly as an air raid siren whines for Allied Aircraft on a daylight bombing raid.*)

Light rises in the block. The inmates have just finished their evening rations. The dented soup pail is standing in its usual place. The inmates are lounging in their bunks, tired out from their daily grind. Louie is sitting on his favourite box chair. Hans sits opposite him on the other box chair busy picking his teeth. Louie is polishing his shoes. After a moment, Brukmann gets out of his bunk and saunters over to Louie. He squats down next to Louie and removes a dirty piece of cloth from his coat. He unwraps the cloth, removes a piece of sausage, hands it to Louie. Brukmann, we see, is barefoot.

BRUKMANN (*Ingratiatingly*) Here, for you. (*Louie snatches it, starts devouring it greedily. Hans, seeing this, stops picking his teeth, turns angrily to Brukmann*)

HANS (*Angrily*) What's that?

BRUKMANN (*Defensively*) Only a piece of liver sausage. (*Hans tries to grab it away from Louie, but Louie quickly stuffs the last piece into his mouth*)

HANS (*To Louie*) Pig! (*Louie swallows it down*)

LOUIE (*Annoyed*) Pig? You're the pig. (*Sneeringly*) You promised me chicken. Huh! What did I get? Nothing. Then you show me gold teeth and you say, tomorrow. Huh! Your tomorrow never comes. (*Tauntingly*) From now on, you and I are finished. No more lovemaking.

HANS (*Crawling*) Sorry! Sorry! Sorry! You're not a pig. (*Pointing to Brukmann*) He is. I meant him, not you. (*Brukmann scowls but says nothing*)

LOUIE Leave him alone. He's just given me food. And besides he's a shoemaker, not a fat, stupid Kapo like you!

HANS (*Hurt, touches Louie's foot*) Say you're not angry. Please Louie, say you're not angry.

LOUIE (*Irritably*) Oh all right. I'm not angry with you. Now leave me alone. (*Hans turns to scowl at Bruckmann*)

HANS (*To Brukmann*) Go back to your bunk. (*Brukmann stalls*)

BRUKMANN (*To Louie*) Can I borrow your shoes for a little while? (*Holds out his hands*)

HANS (*Fiercely*) No! Go! (*Brukmann reels back*)

LOUIE   (*To Hans*) They're mine, not yours. (*To annoy Hans, he hands the shoes to Brukmann, who accepts them smilingly*) Only for a few minutes.

HANS   (*Not to be outdone*) Ten minutes. (*Brukmann goes over to his bunk. Puts on the shoes, stands feeling them on his feet, moving his toes around inside them. A look of happiness on his face*)

HANS   (*Contemptuously*) Stupid Dutchman. (*Louie removes his boots*)

LOUIE   (*Massaging his feet*) That stuff they gave me at the revier is no good. Look, my feet are still swollen. (*Hans not only looks, he takes Louie's feet tenderly in his hands and begins to kiss them*)

LOUIE   (*Laughingly*) Stop it Hans! It tickles. (*Hans pays no notice, he kisses and kisses and kisses. Suddenly the door crashes open. Two SS guards with rifles rush in (The two briefed by Kramer) accompanied by two burly Kapos. Every inmate freezes in terror. Brukmann stands transfixed, wearing Louie's shoes. The Kapos wield their truncheons menacingly.*)

FIRST GUARD   (*Barks*) Schnell! Schnell! Everybody out! (*The inmates begin quickly to climb out of their bunks. Hans puts a protective arm across Louie's shoulders. He instinctively knows what's in store*)

AN INMATE   (*Bravely*) Where are we going?

SECOND GUARD   Health examination. Typhus.

ANOTHER INMATE   (*Confused*) At night? (*A Kapo steps forward, raises his truncheon menacingly, the inmate quickly shuts up. The Kapos shove the inmates into line. One SS guard*) *comes over to Hans and Louie, who now stand quietly awaiting their fate.*)

SS GUARD (*Shoving Hans and Louie*) You too! (*Hans takes Louie tenderly by the hand. The inmates begin to file out. Brukmann is last in line. He is about to take off Louie's shoes and call out to him but the SS Guard grabs him by the shoulder, whips him around. All the inmates are now just about out, but Louie manages a glance back at Brukmann wearing his shoes. Guard barks at Brukmann*) Not you! (*Brukmann looks confused. He is about to mouth 'why not me?' But now the guard pushes him away.*) Go back to your bunk and take off your shoes. Wait until the morning. Someone will come for you. You are to be transferred to the Kommandant's vegetable garden. (*Barks*) Now raus! Raus! Get away! (*Brukmann moves away. The guard goes and shuts the door behind him with a bang. Voices, mixed, loud and noisy are heard outside as the Kapos and guards order the inmates to march to the waiting trucks to take them to Birkenau and extermination. Brukmann, smiling, very slowly removes Louie's shoes. Holds them in his hands for a moment, then kisses each shoe in turn.*)

BRUKMANN (*Happily to audience*) My shoes now. (*The light very slowly fades as a smiling Brukmann, unable to believe his good fortune, repeats:* The Kommandant's vegetable garden . . . The Kommandant's vegetable garden . . . Ag so . . .! (*Trucks are heard in the distance. Engines revving. Voices. Commands. Dogs barking.*)

Light rises again in the Steiner household living room. A few moments pass,

107

then Steiner Snr. enters carrying a large cardboard box. He wears a dressing gown over pyjamas and slippers. He places the box on the coffee table, then he places the used cups and saucers and coffee urn on the tray, checks the sugar, leaves the sugar bowl (it is still full), lifts the tray and goes. A few moments pass, then Steiner Jnr. enters. His is casually dressed. He notices that the coffee urn and cups have been removed, so he decides to sit down. Curious about the box, he lifts the lid. He sees that the box contains numerous documents. Thinking that his father has brought the box out because his diary is amongst the documents, he decides to take a look and proceeds to remove the documents. He removes a pile and places them beside the box on the coffee table, but one document falls on the carpet. He ignores it for a moment as he has now found his diary. He flips through it, stopping to read an entry here and there. He comes upon the entry detailing his confession about Fritz and for a while reads the entry. We hear him say, 'Poor Fritz. Poor, beloved Fritz'. He shuts the diary quickly, not wishing to be reminded too starkly again of all the anguish and heartache the memories are bringing back. He shoves the diary under the pile of documents and is about to lift them up and place them back into the box when his eye catches the document on the carpet. He bends down to retrieve it. Something about the document interests him. He begins to read. As he reads, his expression changes to one of utter horror. Just then Steiner Snr. enters carrying the tray with clean cups, saucers and fresh coffee.

STEINER SNR. (*Placing tray down on coffee table*) Helga phoned. She won't be in today. She has to take her cat to the veterinarian. So I brewed us fresh coffee. Later I will make some breakfast. (*Sits down, prepares cups and saucers*) Thank heaven, the phones are working again.

STEINER JNR. (*Holds document up*) Father, this document, it's a legal document covering a change of name. (*Reads*) It states that our surname was changed from Steinowitz to Steiner. Steinowitz is a Jewish name, is it not?

STEINER SNR.   (*Suddenly angry*) Put it away! Put it Away! Why have you gone through my papers behind my back? (*Reaches for the document, but Steiner Jnr. pulls it back out of reach*)

STEINER JNR.   (*Calmly*) Don't you think you owe me an explanation? Haven't *you* done something behind my back? Come, father, the truth.

STEINER SNR.   (*Stunned*) How can you speak to me like this? I'm your father. Or have you forgotten? Give me that document.

STEINER JNR.   (*Firmly*) No, father, not until you explain what this is about. (*Very slight pause*) It's not going to go away, father. The cat is out of the bag. (*Very slight pause. Steiner Snr. shifts very uncomfortably. He tries to lift a cup to pour coffee but his hands shake and he abandons the attempt. He cannot look Steiner Jnr. in the eye*) Do you want me to put the pieces together, or are you . . .? (*Pause*)

STEINER SNR.   (*Heavily*) Is it important? Is it important to drag up the past?

STEINER JNR.   Yes, father, it is. (*Fairly long pause. Steiner Jnr. pours a cup of coffee for his father*) Here, father, have this. (*Steiner Snr. waves it away. He is very upset, his whole body feels flushed and he fidgets, his hands shake so badly that he clasps them together to stop.*) Why did you change our family name, father? Because we are Jews, is that why? (*Pause*)

STEINER SNR.   (*Agonising with guilt*) Yes. (*Shakily he rubs his*

temples, head bowed, he breathes hard as emotions
flood through him)

STEINER JNR. (*Slowly, patiently*) What made you do it? Were
you ashamed of your race? Was it fear? Surely,
father things were not so bad when I was three
years old? That's some twenty-five years ago.
There were no Nazis then. Have we been living
a lie to ourselves all these years? (*Pause*)

STEINER SNR. (*With great difficulty, begins to explain*) It was your
mother. She believed that a Jewish name would
be a stumbling block. Her career meant everything. I wasn't happy about it. But I loved her
so. I would have done anything if it made her
happy. (*Reminisces*) She was such a brilliant pianist.
So rich in talent. (*His voice falters. Steiner Jnr. waits
sympathetically for him to recover*) She had the world
waiting for her. The contracts were flooding in
from all over Europe. (*He wipes a tear, sadly*) She
was so beautiful . . . (*Pause*)

STEINER JNR. (*With great depth of feeling*) I have the blood of
my people on my hands. (*He tosses the document
aside*) These fingers (*opens his hands, palms up-
wards, looks down at them*) have pulled the trigger
so many times. Snuffed out the lives of my own
kind. (*Pause, then heavily*) And now . . . Auschwitz! (*He rises angrily*) For the love of God, father!
You denied me what I am! What have you
done?!

STEINER SNR. (*Grasping desperately for empathy*) I did it for her.
I did it for her career. (*He looks up in desperation*)

STEINER JNR. (*Disgusted*) A career comes before a birthright!?

Can't you see what you have done? For half a lifetime you have led a lie and made me a bastard of my own blood!

SEINER SNR. (*Pleading*) No! No! I didn't want it that way. I wanted us to be happy. To belong. To prosper. It was an act of love. Love for you. Love for your mother. I did it for you and her. (*Steiner Jnr. closes his eyes momentarily, shakes his head*)

STEINER JNR. (*Quietly*) No, father. It wasn't an act of love. Not for me, not for mother, not for anyone else. It was the act of a man who denied what he was. (*Pause*) All these years I've lived thinking day and night what a coward I am. What a coward I am, letting my best friend drown in that ice-cold black water. But now – now I find that I am not alone. We are two of a kind, father. You know the old saying, a chip off the old block. Well, father, the truth is we are both cowards, aren't we? You and me, two of a kind.

STEINER SNR. (*Pathetically*) Am I to blame now for everything? For the Einsatzgruppen? For Auschwitz?

STEINER JNR. (*Gently*) No, father, you are only to blame for yourself. A Jew who denies his blood. (*Very slight pause, then sadly*) As for myself, the moment of truth has arrived. My life has been nothing but a lie. A deception of myself. Nothing but a shadow in a mirror. (*Sighs deeply, then with great feeling*) Perhaps if I had known the truth, I would have let my anger find another way. But now, now, it's too late. (*Philosophically*) Perhaps that was my destiny. Who will ever know . . .?

(*Steiner Snr. gets up, comes over to his son, tries to embrace him, but Steiner Jnr. shies away*) No, father. Not anymore.

STEINER SNR. (*Emotionally shattered*) Don't – please don't. You've all I have. (*Desperately*) Go to Himmler. Get out of Auschwitz. Just stay. Don't report back. The war has made so much confusion. They will never find you. We can find another place. We can move to the country where you will be safe. (*Pause*)

STEINER JNR. (*Quietly*) I've been hiding all my life, father. Hiding from my race – my blood – my birthright – myself. And now, father, you want me to go on hiding?

STEINER SNR. (*Pleading*) I'm old. Do it for me. (*Very slight pause*) Please, I beg you. (*Their eyes meet for a moment. Pause*)

STEINER JNR. (*With deep feeling*) In spite of everything, father, I love you. (*He moves to go*)

STEINER SNR. (*Breaking down, weeping*) Don't go . . .! (*Steiner Jnr. moves to his father, places his hands on the weeping old man's shoulders*)

STEINER JNR. (*Very gently*) My leave ends today, father. I have to pack. My train leaves in two hours. (*He quickly goes. Steiner Snr. shuffles over to his armchair, sits down, buries his head in his hands, grief stricken. The light slowly fades*)

Light rises slowly in Hoess's office. Hoess is sitting behind his desk. A pile of files lies in front of him. He is sitting back slightly, reading one of them. A few moments pass, then the door opens and the duty corporal comes in, remains standing close to the door. Hoess looks up at the corporal.

Shoes

HOESS (*Irritably*) Ja, what is it? (*Slams down the file*)

DUTY CORPORAL Lieutenant Möller wishes to see you, Herr Kommandant.

HOESS (*Testily*) Later, I'm busy. (*The corporal is about to go when Hoess changes his mind*) Ach, all right, send him in. (*Voices off: 'The Kommandant says it's in order. Go in please Lieutenant Möller.' Möller enters, comes over to Hoess, stands in front of his desk. They exchange salutes*)

MÖLLER (*Fawning*) Thank you for giving me your time, Herr Kommandant. (*Stands dutifully*)

HOESS (*With forced politeness*) What can I do for you, Lieutenant Möller? (*Taps his fingers on the desk*)

MÖLLER I have a suggestion to make Herr Kommandant.

HOESS (*Interested*) Yes?

MÖLLER (*Enthusiastically, earnestly*) Cannot we change the sign above the entrance to Auschwitz to read: Arbeit macht frei vir Deutschland? Or better still, Arbeit macht frei vir Adolf Hitler? (*Hoess's jaw muscles tighten*)

HOESS (*With forced pleasantness*) Ja. Good idea, Möller. I shall forward your suggestion to Berlin. Anything else? You must excuse me, Möller, but as you can see, there is a lot of paperwork to do.

MÖLLER No, that is all. Thank you, Herr Kommandant. (*Hoess nods, forces a smile. They exchange salutes, Möller goes. As the door shuts, Hoess snatches up the phone, dials a number, barks into receiver.*)

HOESS (*Loudly*) Bring me a bottle of schnapps! No, make it two! (*He slams down the phone. To himself:*)

Surrounded by idiots! Idiots! (*Furiously*) Millions of Jews to be taken care of. I must worry about a sign! (*Unhappily*) My teeth ache day and night. (*He rubs them. The door opens. The duty corporal enters carrying two bottles of scotch. Places them on Hoess's desk*)

DUTY CORPORAL (*Apologetically*) Schnapps is out of stock, Herr Kommandant. Only English whisky.

HOESS (*Impatiently*) Ja gut. No more visitors, Corporal. (*He lifts a bottle, reads the label. Duty corporal exits. He puts down the bottle, opens a drawer and takes out a glass, uncaps the bottle, pours himself a half glass, sips pleasurably. Voices off are heard. A loud argument follows, then protests, then the door opens and Kleinsmidt barges in, ignoring the heated words of the duty corporal, who protests that the Kommandant does not wish to be disturbed. Hoess looks up, sees that it's Kleinsmidt, waves the duty corporal away*) Ah, Kleinsmidt! (*Kleinsmidt goes over to Hoess's desk. They exchange salutes. Hoess motions to Kleinsmidt to sit. Kleinsmidt removes his cap, sits on edge of the chair, leaning on the desk.*)

KLEINSMIDT (*Gravely*) Bad news.

HOESS What is it?

KLEINSMIDT Steiner is dead. Shot himself.

HOESS (*Shocked*) When?! How?!

KLEINSMIDT (*Explaining slowly, more relaxed now*) Steiner returned from leave last night. He went straight to his quarters. Around midnight, one of the duty guards saw Kramer visiting his room. Half an hour later the guard saw Kramer leave. An hour later he heard a shot, but dismissed it as coming from Steiner's quarters. When Steiner did not report to me this morning, I went to his room. (*Pause*)

HOESS (*Perplexed*) Why? Why did he blow his brains out?

KLEINSMIDT (*Shrugs*) I cannot find a reason.

HOESS (*Deeply concerned*) Did you speak to Kramer? (*Worried*) What does he say? Does he know why Steiner would do such a thing?

KLEINSMIDT I spoke with Kramer for over an hour. He could offer no reason. (*Pause*)

HOESS (*Worried*) What do we tell Berlin? Suicide of one of my officers. It won't look good on my record. (*Pause*) What do we do, Kleinsmidt?

KLEINSMIDT (*Indicates bottle of scotch*) May I?

HOESS (*Generously*) Of course. Help yourself. (*Hoess opens a drawer, removes a second glass, places it in front of Kleinsmidt*) Pour a big one. You need it. (*Kleinsmidt pours almost to the brim*)

HOESS (*Raising his glass*) Well then, to Steiner.

KLEINSMIDT (*Raises his glass*) To Steiner. (*They gulp some whisky.*)

HOESS (*Wiping his mouth on the back of his hand.*) Will you arrange the funeral?

KLEINSMIDT Yes.

HOESS Full military honours. Afterwards, drinks and food for all officers at my house. Frau Hoess will see to it. (*Very slight pause*) We cannot allow morale to go down.

KLEINSMIDT Leave it to me. (*They drink*)

HOESS (*Rubbing his chin, still extremely concerned*) Berlin will have to be notified. Steiner is not just a dog off the street. Questions will be asked. (*He rubs his teeth*) All this makes my teeth ache. Jews! Jews! Jews! Now Steiner killing himself! (*He downs his scotch, pours another, gulps it greedily*) This isn't a walk in the park, Kleinsmidt. It can effect my promotion. (*Now he drinks straight from the bottle*)

KLEINSMIDT (*Reassuringly*) Perhaps Berlin doesn't need to know everything. (*Schemingly*) Perhaps we don't have to give all the facts – just some.

HOESS What are you saying?

KLEINSMIDT (*Grins*) An accident. (*Shrugs*) Nobody saw it. We say he was cleaning his Walther. It went off accidentally. We can arrange for the autopsy report to confirm it. (*He pours more scotch, topping up his glass*)

HOESS (*A bit boozy now*) Why not? (*Rubs his teeth again, more vigorously this time*) Ja. Why not? An accident. Of course, Kleinsmidt, a simple accident! (*Pause*) No one in Berlin will query an accident. A suicide, yes. But an accident, no. Good thinking, Kleinsmidt. Ja, very good thinking.

KLEINSMIDT Will you telephone his father? (*Very slight pause. They drink, Hoess opens the second bottle of scotch.*)

HOESS (*Pouring scotch from the new bottle*) No. No, let Berlin do it. Steiner's family is too high up. His father will not like a Kommandant giving him the news. A general, yes, but not me.

(They drink. Both are now showing signs of getting drunk)

KLEINSMIDT   Did you know anything about his family?

HOESS   No, not really. I know, of course, that his mother played the piano at the Führer's birthday party. And that Reichsführer Himmler and Steiner's father were old pals. *(Sighs, almost reverently)* Such good Germans. *(Drinks)* Pity about Steiner . . . good Aryan stock.

KLEINSMIDT   A strange man. I never really got to know Steiner. He was always – so, so – distant.

HOESS   *(Re-thinking their plan, doubts creeping in)* The bullet – did it go straight into his head?

KLEINSMIDT   Yes straight in.

HOESS   Will an accident stick?

KLEINSMIDT   *(Confidently)* Of course. If necessary, we can quite easily make the necessary changes. We have some good doctors here. Dr Mengele will always oblige you. After all, look at all the guinea pigs you provide. *(They laugh)*

HOESS   *(Drunkenly)* My teeth ache. *(He rubs them)*

KLEINSMIDT   *(Getting up, a bit unsteadily)* I will start on the report for Berlin.

HOESS   *(Staring up at Kleinsmidt with boozy looks)* You want to know something, Kleinsmidt? Something very interesting? Something special?

KLEINSMIDT   *(Curious)* Yes. What Herr Kommandant?

HOESS   *(Contentedly drunk)* In Auschwitz – we always find a reason for everything.

KLEINSMIDT (*Fervently*) Heil Hitler! (*Hoess half rises*)

HOESS (*Drunkenly*) Heil Hitler! (*They exchange sloppy salutes. Kleinsmidt goes, marches out with very controlled steps. Door shuts noisely. Hoess sags into his chair, pours another glass of scotch, slopping it over the desk. The shunting and coupling of trains is heard far off at first, then the sounds grow slowly, progressively, louder. Hoess rubs his teeth. Dogs bark. Commands are shouted. Voices. Children crying. Hoess gulps his scotch. His head drops. He falls asleep. The glass drops from his hand. The light very slowly fades.*)